Praise for

MEDIOCRACY

"If we live in an age where gasbags and show-offs increasingly walk the halls of power, Alain Deneault's brilliant and witty book reveals the truth behind the grandstanding: a crushing and intolerant mediocracy. The extreme average is now the new normal. You know who they are. The brainless politician who acts on a 'hunch'. Professors who can't teach without hundreds of pointless PowerPoint slides. Business managers who have absolutely no idea what they're talking about. Painfully average students. Deneault's book is essential reading for anyone today who still cares about escaping the insipid banality of neoliberal capitalism."

— PETER FLEMING, author of *The Death of Homo Economicus: Work, Debt and the Myth of Endless Accumulation*

"The nature of domination in our society is precisely imprecise, creating a challenge for the middle theories we use to make sense of living amid the shiny ruins of late stage capitalism. This book advances a theory grand enough for the task of piercing that veil."

— TRESSIE MCMILLAN COTTOM, assistant professor of sociology, Virginia Commonwealth University

MEDIOCRACY

The Politics of the Extreme Centre

Alain Deneault

Translated by Catherine Browne

Between the Lines
Toronto

Mediocracy

Originally published in French as *La médiocratie* © Lux Éditeur, Montreal, 2015
and *politiques de l'extrême centre* © Lux Éditeur, Montreal, 2016
www.luxediteur.com

English translation © 2018 Catherine Browne

First published in English translation in 2018 by
Between the Lines
401 Richmond Street West, Studio 281
Toronto, Ontario M5V 3A8 Canada
1-800-718-7201
www.btlbooks.com

Library and Archives Canada Cataloguing in Publication

Deneault, Alain, 1970-, author
    Mediocracy ; The politics of the extreme centre / Alain Deneault ; translated by Catherine Browne.

Translation of: La médiocratie and Politiques de l'extrême centre.
Includes bibliographical references.
Issued in print and electronic formats.

ISBN 978-1-77113-343-2 (softcover).—ISBN 978-1-77113-344-9 (EPUB).—
ISBN 978-1-77113-345-6 (PDF)

1. Elite (Social sciences).   2. Common good.   3. Social norms.   4. Critical thinking.
5. Civilization—21st century.   6. Mediocrity.   I. Deneault, Alain, 1970–.   Médiocratie. English.
II. Deneault, Alain, 1970–.   Politiques de l'extrême centre. English.
III. Title.   IV. Title: Politics of the extreme centre.

HM1263.D4613 2018   303.3'4   C2017-907774-0
C2017-907775-9

Front cover design and illustration by Jack Dylan
Text design by Gordon Robertson
Printed in Canada

RECYCLED
Paper made from
recycled material
FSC® C103567

We acknowledge for their financial support of our publishing activities: the Government of Canada; the Canada Council for the Arts, which last year invested $153 million to bring the arts to Canadians throughout the country; and the Government of Ontario through the Ontario Arts Council, the Ontario Book Publishers Tax Credit program, and the Ontario Media Development Corporation.

We acknowledge the financial support of the Government of Canada through the National Translation Program for Book Publishing, an initiative of the *Roadmap for Canada's Official Languages 2013-2018: Education, Immigration, Communities*, for our translation activities.

Canada Council
for the Arts

Conseil des Arts
du Canada

Canadä

ONTARIO ARTS COUNCIL
CONSEIL DES ARTS DE L'ONTARIO
an Ontario government agency
un organisme du gouvernement de l'Ontario

CONTENTS

TRANSLATOR'S NOTE

It has been a great pleasure to translate Alain Deneault's fierce, funny, and thought-provoking book into English.

A French reader's expectations of this book would be shaped by the category to which it belongs, the *essai*, which has no exact equivalent in English. This category embraces a wide variety of publications: Simone de Beauvoir's *The Second Sex* is an *essai*, as are Roland Barthes's *Mythologies*, Guy Debord's *The Society of the Spectacle*, and Henri Lefebvre's *The Right to the City*. Theodor Adorno's *Minima Moralia* is an example in German. The books I have just named are intellectually serious and politically engaged. Their style is lively and sometimes polemical; they were written for educated readers, but not specifically for academics. Writing in this genre, authors are not required to avoid subjectivity, footnote everything, or stick to a specialized subject they have studied for decades. They are allowed to range over multiple disciplines and to put forward abstract ideas using difficult philosophical terms. These characteristics, which would not necessarily attract attention in French, may be somewhat unexpected in English. (I have provided the endnotes that were not included in the French edition; a reader who chooses to ignore them will be experiencing the book as it was written.)

In many ways this translation is different from the original French. With the author's consent, some sections have been removed, and others rewritten, to sharpen the book's focus on issues of relevance to an English-language audience. In this respect, there has been a significant effort to adapt the book.

At the same time, I was reluctant to make the book sound as if it had been written in standard North American English. Deneault's style, deeply rooted in the French aesthetic, shapes his way of thinking and creating meaning. To remove every unusual aspect of this style would be to negate the specific quality of his thought. I have tried to convey this quality, and my hope is that readers will find pleasure in discovering something that is recognizably written in English, yet remains radically strange.

Catherine Browne

INTRODUCTION

P UT THOSE COMPLEX tomes aside: an accounting textbook will do the job. Don't be proud, or witty, or even at ease: you'll come across as arrogant. Stop being so passionate: you'll scare people off. Most importantly, avoid "good ideas": the shredder is full of them. That piercing look of yours makes people anxious: open your eyes and relax your lips. Your thoughts should be flabby, and they should look flabby, too. When you talk about yourself, make sure we know you're nothing much. That will help us put you in the right box. Times have changed. No one stormed the Bastille, there was no Reichstag fire, the *Aurora* did not fire a shot. And yet the attack was launched, and it worked: the mediocre have taken power.

What is the chief skill of a mediocre person? Recognizing another one. Together, they will organize back-scratchings, make sure favours are returned, and, since they quickly find ways to attract their fellows, establish the power of a growing clan. What really matters is not avoiding stupidity, but making sure it is decorated with images of power. "If stupidity did not outwardly resemble progress, genius, hope, and improvement, the chances are that no one would want to be stupid," observed Robert Musil.[1] Be comfortable hiding your shortcomings behind a normal attitude, always claim to be pragmatic, and be ready to improve yourself—for mediocracy suffers neither inability nor incompetence. You should know how to use the software, fill out a form without whining, parrot phrases such as "high standards of corporate governance" and "value proposition," and say hello to the right people at the right time. But—and this is key—you must not go any further.

"Mediocrity" designates what is average, just as "superiority" and "inferiority" designate what is superior or inferior. As a concept, "averageness" has little currency. But "mediocrity" does not refer to the average as an abstraction—it is the average stage in actuality; and "mediocracy," therefore, is the average when it has been granted authority. Mediocracy establishes an order in which the average is no longer an abstract synthesis that allows us to grasp the state of things, but the standard that we are compelled to obey. And if we assert our freedom, that simply demonstrates how effective the system is.

The division and industrialization of labour—both manual and intellectual—have greatly contributed to the advent of mediocre power. Perfecting each task to make it useful to a whole that no one can grasp has helped make experts out of gasbags who spout just-in-time orations on fragments of truth, while workers are reduced to tools for whom "life-activity . . . is but a means of securing [their] own existence."[2]

Such was Marx's observation in 1849, and he also noted that capital, in reducing labour first to labour power, then to an abstract unit of measure, and finally to its cost (salary being equivalent to what workers need to reproduce their labour power), has made workers indifferent to work itself. Craftsmanship has been lost. People may now produce meals on the assembly line without knowing how to cook at home, give customers instructions over the phone that they don't understand themselves, sell books or newspapers that they themselves never read. Pride in a job well done is vanishing. As Marx explained in the *Contribution to the Critique of Political Economy* (1857):

The fact that the particular kind of labour employed is immaterial is appropriate to a form of society in which individuals easily pass from one type of labour to another, the particular type of labour being accidental to them and therefore irrelevant. Labour, not only as a category but in reality, has become a means to create wealth in general.[3]

Devitalized labour, seen by the worker as "but a means of securing his own existence," is the means that capital has given itself to ensure its own growth. Employers and workers are agreed at least on one thing: every craft has become a job, and every job is seen as a "means."

Languages derived from Latin tend to use similar words for the average and for something used to reach a goal: French: *moyenne / moyen*, Italian: *media / mezzo*, Spanish: *promedio / medio*. In English, the "mean" is the midpoint between two opposites, and the word describing a way of attaining a goal is almost the same: "means." We say that work becomes a mere *means* when it is calibrated as a *mean* input, and this is neither a pun nor a simple lexical coincidence. When every action is required to comply with the average mode, society as a whole is confined to triviality. In French, the words for means / mean (*moyen / moyenne*) are also etymologically related to the word *milieu*, which means both environment and middle, and can specifically denote the professional milieu as a locus of (sometimes dishonest) compromise in which no true work, *œuvre*, can take place.

It should be pointed out, however, that mediocre people are not lying around doing nothing: they know how to work hard. Much effort is required to produce a large-scale television show, apply for a research grant, design an aerodynamic-looking yogourt jar, or organize the ritual content of a meeting between a minister and a delegation of her counterparts. Not everyone has the means to reach these ends. Technical perfection is needed to conceal the profound intellectual laziness involved in so many conformist professions of faith. Committed to the exacting demands of work that is never their own, and immersed in thoughts that are ordered from above, mediocre people lose sight of their own banality.

Progress cannot be stopped. The mediocre were once thought to be a minority. For La Bruyère, the mediocre person was a vile creature who used his knowledge of gossip and intrigue among the powerful to take advantage of every situation.

> Celse is of mediocre standing, but those of high standing put up with him; he is not learned, but he is acquainted with some learned men; he has little merit, but he knows people who have a great deal of it; he has no abilities, but he has a tongue that serves him to be understood and feet that carry him from one place to another.[4]

Once they become dominant, the Celses of this world have no one to imitate but themselves. Power is something that they acquire, almost without knowing what they are doing. Their systems of supervision, undeserved privilege, complacency, and collusion ultimately bring them to the head of institutions.

This phenomenon has been denounced in every generation. Gustave Flaubert quoted the notebooks of his friend, the poet Louis Bouilhet:

> O fetid mediocracy, utilitarian poetry, literature of underlings, aesthetic prattling, economic vomit, scrofulous products of an exhausted nation, I loathe you with the full power of my soul! You are not gangrene, you are atrophy! You are not the hot, red phlegmon of feverish eras, but a cold, pale-bordered abscess dripping from its source in some deep cavity![5]

However, these are still denunciations of impostures and infatuations: what is being unmasked is an ineffectual will to greatness, not, as yet, a system that is satisfied with littleness and actually requires such satisfaction.

Laurence J. Peter and Raymond Hull were among the first to bear witness to the spread of mediocrity throughout an entire system. Their thesis in *The Peter Principle*, developed in the postwar years, is relentless in its clarity: systemic processes help those who have average levels of competence rise to positions of power, pushing aside both the supercompetent and the incompetent. Striking examples of this phenomenon are found in schools. Schools will dismiss a teacher who cannot follow a schedule and knows nothing about his subject matter, but they will also reject a rebel who makes major changes to teaching protocols in order to bring a class with learning disabilities to a point where they score better in reading and arithmetic than children in regular classes. And they will eliminate an unconventional teacher whose pupils finish two or three years' work in one year. According to Peter and Hull, in this last case, the teacher was blamed for disrupting the official marking system, and especially for causing "severe anxiety to the teacher who would next year have to handle the children who had already covered the work."[6] Such is the process shaping the "secondary illiterate,"[7] to use a phrase coined by Hans Magnus Enzensberger. This new subject, mass-produced by teaching and research institutions, is proud to possess a store of useful knowledge that does not lead her to question its ideological underpinnings.

Enzensberger describes the secondary illiterate as follows: "He considers himself to be well informed, can decode instructions, pictograms, and checks, and moves in a world that seals him off from every challenge to his confidence."[8] Mediocre scholars do not think for themselves: for the purposes of career advancement, they delegate their power of thought to a superior authority who dictates their strategies. Self-censorship is obligatory and must be presented as an artful trick.

Since the publication of *The Peter Principle*, the tendency to banish the non-mediocre has been regularly confirmed, and today, we have reached a point where mediocrity is actually recommended. Psychologists who are fully at home in business schools turn value relationships on their head, identifying specific forms of competence as an excess of "self-control." Christy Zhou Koval of the Fuqua School of Business at Duke University, lead author of an article entitled "The Burden of Responsibility: Interpersonal Costs of High Self-Control,"[9] presents workers who place high demands on themselves as subjects who are in some sense responsible for the abuse they will eventually experience. It is up to them to learn to restrict their activity to a narrow framework. Their propensity for well-done work and strong sense of responsibility are seen as a problem. They are failing to work toward their so-called personal objectives, i.e., their career as defined by their custodial institutions.

Mediocracy, then, is the word for a mediocre order that is set up as a model. Russian logician Alexander Zinoviev has described the Soviet regime in terms that bring out its resemblance with our liberal democracies. "It is the mediocre who survive" and "mediocrity has a better chance of succeeding," as the Dauber reflects in *The Yawning Heights*, the satirical novel Zinoviev published in defiance of Soviet authorities in 1976. Theorems put forward in the novel by the Neurasthenic and the Careerist include the following:

> I'm talking about mediocrity as the general average, and not about success in specific area of work, but about social success. These are very different things. . . . If an institution begins to work noticeably better than others, it draws attention to itself. If it is officially recognised in this role, it soon turns into a fake or a showplace, which also in time degenerates into a run-of-the-mill fake.[10]

The rule of mediocrity leads people to carry out an imitation of work that produces the illusion of an outcome. Faking it becomes a value in itself. Mediocracy compels us to subordinate our deliberation to arbitrary models promoted by the authorities. Today, symptoms include a politician explaining to voters that they must submit to Wall Street shareholders, a professor judging a student's paper "too theoretical and too scientific" when it goes beyond the premises set out in a PowerPoint presentation, a film producer insisting that a celebrity be given a starring role in a documentary that she has nothing to do with, or an expert demonstrating his "rationality" by holding forth on (irrational) economic growth. Zinoviev was already aware of feigned work as a psychological force with the power to shape minds:

The imitation of work needs only an apparent result—or rather the mere possibility of justifying the time that has been spent: checking and evaluation of results are carried out by people who've taken part in the imitation, who are connected with it and have an interest in perpetuating it.[11]

A complicit smirk seems to be characteristic of those who share in this power. Believing themselves smarter than everyone else, they take pleasure in words of wisdom such as "You have to play the game." The game—an expression whose vagueness is perfectly suited to mediocre thought—requires you at different times to obsequiously comply with rules established for the sole purpose of occupying a key location on the social chessboard, or to smugly elude these rules, while saving appearances, through acts of collusion that pervert the integrity of the process.

A naive expression such as "playing the game" is a salve for the conscience of fraudulent actors. Following this smiling injunction, pharmaceutical companies ensure that prostate cancers are cured at great expense, even though patients are not expected to face a serious problem until the age of 130, and physicians provide useless treatments knowing that by contract they are compensated for each of their medical acts. With the same nudge-nudge, wink-wink attitude, tax agents who are well equipped to zero in on parties guilty of major economic fraud prefer to hound waitresses who fail to declare their tips. Police officers put an end to investigations as soon as they realize they are shadowing people who belong to the premier's inner circle, and journalists reproduce the tendentious language of press releases issued by the powerful, swimming blindly in the currents of historical movements that they prefer not to think about.

A new recruit to the professoriate is subjected to intimidating initiation rites designed to make her understand that market dynamics prevail over public institutions' founding principles, which should be bypassed. The game may involve transforming home daycare centres managed with state support into businesses that are unconcerned about what happens to children, providing new employees with a workshop where they will learn to deceive each other as part of their personal relations, or playing on an employee's feelings with statements like "Your identity is an asset that belongs to us." Collectively, playing the game means acting as if it doesn't matter that we are playing Russian roulette, staking our all, or staking our life. We're just playing, it's funny, it's light-hearted, it's not for real, it's just a big sham—that's why we're roaring with perverse laughter. The game we are supposed to play is always presented, with a wink, as a ploy that we may criticize to some extent, but whose authority we nonetheless accept. At the same time, we are careful never to make explicit the overall rules of the game, because these rules are entwined with strategies that are most often personal and arbitrary, not to say abusive. In the minds of people who think they are clever, duplicity and cheating are set up as an implicit game at the expense of those they believe are fools. Playing the game, though you may pretend otherwise, means submitting to nothing but the law of greed. This way of thinking reverses our relation to opportunism by defining it as something foreign to the self, but required by society.

The central figure of mediocracy is, of course, the "expert" with whom the majority of today's academics identify. His thought is never quite his own; it belongs to an order of reasoning which, although embodied in him, is driven by specific interests. The expert's function is to transform ideological propositions and sophisms into objects of knowledge that appear to be pure. This is why we can expect no original or strong proposition from him. Above all—and this is the chief criticism levelled at him by Edward Said in the 1993 Reith lectures—this contemporary sophist, who is paid to think in a certain way, is not motivated by the curiosity of an amateur: he doesn't care about the thing he talks about, but acts within a strictly mechanical framework. According to Said, "The particular threat to the intellectual today, whether in the West or in the non-Western world, is not the academy, nor the suburbs, nor the appalling commercialism of journalism and publishing houses, but rather an attitude that I will call professionalism."[12] Professionalization presents itself as an implicit contract between, on the one hand, the various producers of knowledge and discourse, and, on the other, owners of capital. The former provide and format, without spiritual engagement, the practical or theoretical data that the latter require to ensure their legitimacy. Edward Said therefore recognizes in the expert the characteristics of the mediocre: always acting according to "what is considered to be proper, professional behaviour—not rocking the boat, not straying outside the accepted paradigms or limits, making yourself marketable and above all presentable, hence uncontroversial and unpolitical and 'objective.'"[13] For those in power, the mediocre person is the average being through whom they can convey their commands and firmly establish their order.

In this social context, public thought inevitably develops a degree of conformism focused—how surprising—on the middle, the centre, the average moment put forward as a political program. The centre is the object of an electoral representation belonging to a vast transversal party whose constituent parts would be indistinguishable if it were not for the fetishes that Freud described as "small differences." The appearance of discord within the transversal party is a matter of symbols rather than premises. It is worth noting the extent to which in institutions of power—such as parliaments, courthouses, financial institutions, government ministries, press rooms, or laboratories—expressions such as "balanced measures," "juste milieu," and "compromise" have become fetishized. We have reached a point where we can no longer even imagine positions far removed from the centre—these being the positions, of course, that (if they existed) would enable us to participate in the highly regarded process of finding balance.

Socially, thought can only exist at the stage that comes before balance. As it gestates, it already begins to locate itself within the boundaries of the average, because the mind is structurally neutralized by a series of centrist words, of which "governance" is both the most insignificant and the most representative example. The system's reality is both harsh and deadly, but its extremism is hidden behind an ornate display of moderation, leading us to forget that extremism is not what is found at the extremities of the left-right political spectrum, but simply intolerance displayed toward everything that is not oneself. Only blandness, greyness, normativity, reproduction, and mindless statements of the obvious are authorized. Under the auspices of mediocracy, poets hang themselves in the corners of their messy apartments, passionately committed scientists develop answers to questions that no one is asking, brilliant industrialists build imaginary temples, and great policy thinkers produce soliloquies in church basements. This is the political order of the extreme centre. Its policies embody not so much a specific location on the left-right axis as the suppression of this axis, which is replaced by a single approach that claims the virtues of truth and logical necessity. This manoeuvre is dressed up in empty words, or worse yet, power is defined by words associated with what it most hates: innovation, participation, merit, and commitment. Those who do not participate in such duplicitous thought are excluded, and this exclusion, of course, is carried out in a mediocre manner, through negation, denial, and resentment. Symbolic violence of this kind is a tried and true approach.

Mediocracy encourages us in every possible way to doze rather than think, to view as inevitable what is unacceptable and as necessary what is revolting. It makes us into idiots. The fact that we think of the world in terms of average variables is understandable; that some people greatly resemble these average figures is obviously the case. But some of us will never accept the silent injunction ordering everyone to become identical to this average figure. The word "mediocracy" has lost the meaning it might have had in the past when it described the power of the middle class. It describes not so much the domination of mediocre people as the state of domination created by mediocre forms themselves, a state of domination that establishes these forms as the currency of meaning and sometimes the key to survival, to the point where those who aspire to something better and lay claim to sovereignty are subject to the empty words generated by mediocracy.

1

"KNOWLEDGE" AND EXPERTISE

A MERICAN JOURNALIST Chris Hedges does not beat about the bush: academics are responsible for our social ills. Whenever we try to probe the reasons behind our collective perils, there they are—cut off from the world, specializing in infinitesimal subfields, having lost the ability to think critically, obsessed with career advancement, and loyal to collegial networks that look exactly like tribes. Research and training carried out in universities are among the causes of problems such as the evolving ecological crisis, income inequalities that create exclusion nationally and globally, our dependence on fossil fuels, overconsumption, planned obsolescence, the way culture has been turned inside out to become the entertainment industry, minds colonized by advertising, the dominance of international finance over the economy, and the instability of the economic system. Are not university faculty, departments, and laboratories "the elite"? Is it not through knowledge acquired or developed at the university, attested to by impressive diplomas, that avant-garde decision-makers and their staff shape and define the world in which we live?

In *Empire of Illusion*, Hedges insists that there is cause for concern, for "elite universities have banished self-criticism. They refuse to question a self-justifying system. Organization, technology, self-advancement, and information systems are the only things that matter."[1] The university is a component of today's industrial, financial, and ideological apparatus; this is the sense in which it can lay claim to a place in the "knowledge economy." Corporations see the university as a publicly funded provider of the personnel and advanced knowledge they need. For $500 million, the Energy Biosciences Institute at UC Berkeley provides British Petroleum with equipment and researchers' work. "BP can shut down another research center and move into a publicly subsidized one," concludes Hedges.[2] In the United States and Canada—undoubtedly the idea will soon gain favour in Europe—universities are named after Rockefeller, campus buildings display the name of Monsanto, research chairs bear the name of Texas Instruments, classrooms once identified by a number are now known as the PricewaterhouseCoopers room, and scholarships are known by the imperishable name of their sponsor, Bosch.

The university's subservient relationship to clients who purchase its serially produced brains is one that Max Weber would have been unable to imagine, even though he was already denouncing, a hundred years ago, the mediocrity into which the university was sinking by subordinating itself to all-pervasive relations of commercial seduction. At the time, the clients were students and course content was the commodity that was supposed to appeal to them. Teachers were willing to compromise themselves to attract students hesitating between competing institutions. This so corrupted the relationship to research that institutional choices, according to Weber, began to be governed by chance. A researcher driven by imperious passion, strong intuition, an all-encompassing imagination, and a feeling for the work could not hope for professional success unless he also displayed a whole other set of gifts that enabled him to navigate the institution's arcane mysteries. By making something essential out of these "external conditions of the academic man's vocation," as Weber described them in 1919, the institution encouraged mediocrity:

It would be unfair to hold the personal inferiority of faculty members or educational ministries responsible for the fact that so many mediocrities undoubtedly play an eminent role at the universities. The predominance of mediocrity is rather due to the laws of human co-operation, especially of the co-operation of several bodies.[3]

What Weber observed was nothing compared to what we are seeing now. Today, students are no longer consumers of the teaching and diplomas offered on campus; they have become the products. The university sells what it makes of them to its new customers, namely, the corporations and other institutions that fund it. The rector of the Université de Montréal clearly believed he was stating the obvious when he claimed, in the fall of 2011, that "brains must be tailored to business needs." True, the university was managed at the time by administrators from the worlds of banking (National Bank), retail pharmacy (Jean Coutu), industry (SNC-Lavalin), natural gas (Gaz Métro), and the media (Power Corporation and Transcontinental), who sat on its decision-making councils and committees of influence. And yet, the Université de Montréal is still largely funded by the state. Surely it was odd for the business plan of this temple of knowledge to suddenly embody aims that resemble those of a mere public broadcaster—for some were struck by the similarity between the rector's declaration and a famous remark made by Patrick Le Lay, CEO of France's TF1 television network, in 2004: "What we sell to Coca-Cola is available human brain time."

A comparable phenomenon was observed by Libero Zuppiroli in Switzerland. When the École polytechnique de Lausanne became the Swiss Institute of Technology Lausanne, he noticed a plethora of strange disciplines that suddenly appeared in the name of innovation, excellence, and productivity. These disciplines, of course, were entirely dedicated to the interests of business. One of them was neurofinance: in his 2010 book *La bulle universitaire*, Zuppiroli explains that this new research sector is intended "to gain a better understanding of the thought processes that lead to commercial transactions."[4]

Institutions use various criteria to assess universities, including the quantitative (faculty members' publications, degrees earned, employment ratio), the fetishistic (ranking of academic journals, trending themes, networks, publications in English), and factors related to publicity (sponsorships, partnerships, media presence). This "governance" of the university is not just empty posturing: it has a deeply corrupting effect. Quebec sociologist Gilles Gagné gives the following example:

> If I invent a way of making square tomatoes, and a company thinks this is great and buys it from me because it's perfect for a square hamburger, am I contributing to education? No. I'm contributing to the education of the guy who is going to work to make square hamburgers for the company that funded research on tomatoes.[5]

Losing your mind

Thought becomes mediocre when researchers do not care about the spiritual relevance of their propositions. Another early twentieth-century German thinker, Georg Simmel, predicted that the fate of researchers who persisted in this attitude would be tragic. When recruited to serve the economy, thought seems fated to embody, in its practice, the flaws of its institution. It has to produce knowledge regardless of cost, and regardless of how this knowledge may resonate in the world. Theory itself becomes inflationistic. Simmel's essay "The Concept and Tragedy of Culture"[6] describes a production imperative so powerful that the mind is no longer able to get its bearings or to speak. Racing out of control, the machine produces value strictly to satisfy the productivism of the apparatus, which no longer has anything to do with the singular act of thinking. The first reason for this is the superabundance of objective elements through which thought is mediated: books, reports, works themselves made up of theories, concepts, and factual data. There is so much to consider that the mind finds itself heavily burdened on the road that would lead it to produce anything. Drowning in a tide of scientific publications, it fears that it will create merely one more element that will make the phenomenon worse. We have moved a long way from the process of knowing, that is, the process of discovering our consciousness and what our mind is capable of through "the happiness of the creative person in his or her work, no matter how great or small it might be." For the creative person, according to Simmel,

> alongside the release of inner tensions, the proof of subjective strength and the satisfaction at having fulfilled a demand, there also exists a kind of objective satisfaction, as it were, at the fact that this work is now in existence—that the cosmos of somehow valuable objects has been enriched by this particular piece.[7]

The process of Hegelian inspiration that Simmel describes is no longer conceivable. We have reached full capacity: the road toward the realization of thought is blocked. Productivism and its process of accumulation have carried the day. The mind's work of slow and intimate assimilation is obstructed by a dizzying proliferation of references. Mediocrity takes over. The researcher, paralyzed as she faces the mountain of references that precede her in the infinite smallness of the question she is expected to pursue, experiences the loss of her mind. There no longer seems to be any point in meditating on what the ancients have done before us in order to add a new piece of work to already existing culture. Instead, we see hordes of scribblers satisfied with taking their turn in producing serial knowledge, without caring about the deeper meaning their work might embody. Simmel gives the example of a well-known philologist putting forward massive amounts of knowledge devoid of any perspective:

Philological technique has been developed, on the one hand, to an unexcelled refinement and perfection, whereas, on the other, the number of objects, which it is of real interest for intellectual culture to treat in that way, do not grow to the same extent, and thus philological effort often becomes a micrology, a pedanticism in the treatment of the unessential—an idle running of the method, as it were, the continuation of the objective norm, the independent path of which no longer coincides with that of culture as a perfection of life. In this way, what could be called superfluous knowledge is accumulating in many areas of scholarship and science. . . . The enormous supply of people willing to engage in intellectual production and often gifted for it, a supply favoured by economic factors, has led to an autonomous evaluation of *all* scholarly work whose value is indeed often only a convention, almost a conspiracy of the scholarly caste.[8]

This is when research enters a tragic phase. The more institutions produce, the more impossible it seems to assimilate their production to make a reasonable contribution, and so the process continues. Cultural production breaks out of its subjective constraints, becoming subordinate to the autonomous imperatives of institutionalized research.

Scholarly opinion makers

Within this economy, the university today no longer sells research results, but strictly its brand, the one that it stamps on reports and to which it owns the rights. This was viewed as an established fact by Edelman, a public relations firm that advised TransCanada—the company that owns the Keystone pipeline—on the creation of a communications plan that would make its proposed Energy East pipeline acceptable to the people of Quebec.

Edelman strategists told TransCanada to fund a Quebec university whose researchers would then describe the project as environmentally safe. According to Edelman, "supporting a major financing campaign" should suffice to obtain these results; the campaign "could help to show how serious TransCanada is about the issues, as well as contribute to a more positive image for the company."[9] The Edelman documents, released by Greenpeace in November 2014,[10] were covered by Radio-Canada and other Quebec media. Not a single university professor, manager, or administrator was heard to denounce the situation or argue the fantastical nature of the hypothesis. University administrators did not feel discredited by the publication of this document, which presented them as corrupt.

Binding themselves to big business and institutions of power, holding nothing back, research institutions are not just selling knowledge to their clients. They are also partners in manipulation. Universities are a key instrument of lobbying firms, despite the highly problematic nature of these firms' practices. It is a mistake to think of lobbying only in terms of canvassing elected officials for their vote. As opinion specialists, lobbyists take a much wider approach: they work to create contexts that will force elected officials to make certain choices, without the lobbyists having to do anything. Seeking to influence reality itself, lobbyists attempt to manufacture a climate that is favourable to their client's interests, and one way of doing this is to publicly mobilize industry-funded "experts" to give a performance. In a personal account published in 2002, career lobbyist Éric Eugène explained that his job was to find multiple ways of reaching a single goal: buying the outcome of a public institution's decision. These multiple ways included corruption, intimidation, manipulation, and investigation. According to Eugène, researchers participating in such games are easily identified. "Where does the expert come from and what is his career plan? Does he work for the public sector? If so, is that where he wants to stay until the end of his career, or would he like to move to the private sector? Who funds the laboratory, whether public or private, where he works? It is clear that the expert is not independent, and that his work must be shaped by the type of funding he receives," writes a repentant Eugène.[11]

Edelman told TransCanada that it would investigate environmental activists opposed to the Energy East pipeline and seek to uncover financial or legal information, with the goal of eventually discrediting them. Edelman also invited TransCanada to organize "popular" pro-oil actions carried out by "activists" who would be directly funded by the company. Another idea was to pay hordes of Internet users to relay the company's message through social media. Had the plan not been leaked to the media, Trans-Canada would also have sought help from Quebec political figures who supported the pipeline, such as Pierre-Marc Johnson, Lucien Bouchard, and Monique Jérôme-Forget. This is the kind of well-orchestrated campaign in which academics are so often expected to play a part. To keep up appearances, all they have to do is to play the game without questioning the overall scheme that they are participating in.

It's dull—it's scientific

The conceit of knowledge managers leads them to believe that they can dominate language: they think they can reduce it to signals that can easily be manipulated to convince their peers to send money their way. A word that is no longer fashionable will be removed from an application; a reference currently on everyone's lips will be emphasized, even if they know nothing about it. In the section of the form where only a limited number of terms can be inserted, they will perform a lexical slalom, careening between hot and cold, angel and devil, venality and ethics, consensus and revolution. And finally, they will assert with a flourish that their attitude will be completely different once the fabled treasure has finally been won. Of course, my grant proposal is nothing but hot air, but just give me the money and I'll show you what I can do! As if we could be stronger than the words we used to make these deals, and were rulers of language instead of being ruled by it. But we have not read Blanchot— we have sidestepped Derrida—we have failed to understand Lacan—we have scorned Kristeva. No sooner have these mercenaries of the word been rewarded for their cowardice than they become harsh and sterile, forgetting critical thinking (on which they have now turned their backs), committed to their business partners as if their life depended on it, and focused on returning favours to their peers, whose applications will rely on the same shared ideological signifiers.

The university has been working for decades now to make itself manipulable by anyone who wants to finance it; to some extent, it may have been doing this since its modern foundation. Hans Magnus Enzensberger recalls the distant origins of the problem in his essay "In Praise of the Illiterate":

> Making the population literate had nothing to do with enlightenment. The philanthropists and priests of culture who championed it were only the accomplices of a capitalist industry that demanded of the state that it make skilled laborers available to it. . . . Quite another type of progress was at stake. It consisted of taming the illiterate, this "lowest class of people," driving out their imagination and their stubbornness, and from this time on exploiting not only their muscle power and their manual skills but their brains as well.[12]

The academic habitus consists in letting yourself be dominated. Academics are in complete disarray, and only money seems to provide their practices with some consistency. They have surrendered, and this shapes their view of how they should use language in research. Academic writing is based on an implicit rule that becomes explicit if anyone breaks it: only a neutral, calm, and measured tone makes one's prose worthy of science. Whenever possible, writing should be dull. Stylistically, writing that lays claim to knowledge must always circle around the middle ground: anything else will cause unease. A distinguished professor will feel apprehensive about a proposition if it is not presented according to the requirements of objective thought. If he recognizes the relevance of an idea, but the way it is crafted strikes him as unsuited to an academic environment, he may eventually repeat it without saying where he got it. For tone is everything.

Tone is related, first of all, to word choice. It is preferable to use words that sound scientific, if only to suggest that your thoughts are not associated with the here and now. Instead of "money," for instance, discuss "currency." Also, you must avoid terms that are charged with emotion as a result of their history: don't say "political revolts," but talk about "resilience"; don't discuss "class," but analyze social "categories." Some even turn their noses up at the expression "tax justice," which is deemed "too political."

Next, it is important not to use crude language to pour scorn on prominent social actors, especially if they are powerful. Multinational corporations come to mind. According to a narrow reading of Max Weber, such an appearance of resentment would undermine your claim to ethical neutrality. To avoid such an unpleasant impression, it is best to avoid the entire lexicon of criminal law and act as if this vocabulary were the sole province of legal scholars. Faced with certain phenomena, speak of "dubious acts" or "bad governance" rather than "crimes" or "plundering." Terms derived from criminal law are exclusively reserved for acts so defined by the courts: the operations of Bernie Madoff, for instance, may be described as "criminal." We must act as if all scientific disciplines were subject to the regional, and highly partial, discipline of law. In doing so, we are ignoring the analysis of sociologist Émile Durkheim, who argued that every field of thought and culture has its own definition of crime.

The normative tone is accompanied by references to well-established concepts: we must stick to the idea of state security or the social contract as defined by tradition, rather than appropriate the controversial ideas of Louise Michel or Herbert Marcuse. We should think about problems in relation to what the world ought to be, focusing on abstract ideas about standards, justice, or communicational ethics, rather than lay the foundations of a conceptual and contextual reflection on what the world is becoming (oligarchy, plutocracy, financial totalitarianism). In French, making up nouns based on the gerund is also a sign of moderation: *migrance, consultance, survivance*, and *gouvernance* are nouns based on migrating, consulting, surviving, and governing. The gerund is a passive tense referring to a state of fact that is devoid of history; once it becomes a noun, it deals with things in a disembodied manner.

And finally, don't name names when actors are involved in illicit undertakings: withholding information shows that you are scientific. No doubt this explains why Canadian universities have failed, in over fifty years, to produce a single thesis on a topic of undeniable importance—the impact on our public institutions of the multibillionaire Desmarais family, which controls a major international financial and media conglomerate (Power Corporation) and has long played a key role in Canadian political life. Meanwhile, any number of arguments have been developed on the abstract standards that ought to be established in the world.

Tone is not just a matter of word choice. It is also related to rhythm. The type of writing that prevails in today's scientific world applies the same lexical structure in all circumstances. To this mode is opposed the "modulation" described by Gilles Deleuze in *Two Regimes of Madness*. Deleuze was referring to Friedrich Nietzsche (a writer no academic would be willing to edit if he were our contemporary) when he wrote that modulation "traces a broken line in perpetual bifurcation, a rhythmic line"[13]—one that enables us to reflect on the contingencies of history, the social vicissitudes, and the other unquantifiable elements throughout which subjects remain, in the last analysis, those who think the world. Tone, as soon as we acknowledge its peculiarity, adapt it to the object, and recognize its imaginative potential, redefines the mould in which thought is shaped. This mode, or mould, must also be invented, inasmuch as we make it into something plastic that is shaped by the work of writing, at the same time as it determines both the shape and the substance of what we are saying. Deleuze calls on Georges Buffon (biologist and author of a famous treatise on style), who formulated an analogy between the appearance of the text and the morphology of an animal, to create the expression "inner mould." Form bears witness to what a body or text is capable of.

Research institutions choose rather to confine themselves to a tightly constrained tone and world. In this superficial environment, a thousand and one details determine whether a theory will be accepted or rejected, including the person's clothing, posture, demeanour, and tone of voice, how quickly they speak, how they regulate intensity, how they associate ideas, the references they choose to quote, and possibly also their accent, origin, gender, and age. This is especially the case in regard to grants and job applications. Narrow formal boundaries contain the proposition in a neurotic sense, guaranteeing that some thoughts will never be uttered.

Who wants things to be done this way, and who benefits from this obligatory tone? One major American sociologist to have addressed this question is, not surprisingly, one of the great stylists of the discipline. In *White Collar: The American Middle Classes*, C. Wright Mills describes "a vague general fear—sometimes called 'discretion' and 'good judgment'—which leads to self-intimidation and finally becomes so habitual that the scholar is unaware of it." This is an effect of the bureaucratization of the scholar's profession; the "agreements of academic gentlemen" exert "manipulative control" over the "insurgent."[14] The prescribed tone prevents academics who adopt it from moving too far away from the dominant ideology's boundaries. Today, this tone is used by the professor/entrepreneur whose customers are located in the corporate world and other institutions of power that need research findings, expert pronouncements, and other symbols. Chris Hedges makes the point more crudely:

> This vocabulary, a sign of the "specialist" and, of course, the elitist, thwarts universal understanding. It keeps the uninitiated from asking unpleasant questions. It destroys the search for the common good. It dices disciplines, faculty, students, and finally experts into tiny, spe-

cialized fragments. It allows students and faculty to retreat into these self-imposed fiefdoms and neglect the most pressing moral, political, and cultural questions.[15]

Writing on the road to ruin

If only this normative tone produced a coherent language. On the contrary, the rules of academic writing degrade students who force themselves to comply with them while they are at the university; they must relearn how to write as soon as they leave the academic world behind.

According to Kristen R. Ghodsee, professor of women's studies at Bowdoin College in Maine, "academics are collectively responsible for the production of some of the most obtuse and impenetrable prose in the English language." Venting online, she writes:

> Rhetorical fashions come and go but the penchant for opacity has become a defining feature of contemporary scholarship. . . . Academese is the secret code that some scholars use to signal that they are members of the club. It ensures that no one can really tell whether their ideas are brilliant, bad, or merely mediocre.[16]

Ghodsee is annoyed by fads such as the rejection of words ending in -ism, which are now passé and must be replaced by words ending in -ality; this appears to represent some fine distinction. She notes the inflationist tendency of terms based on the suffix of the day—the study of social and political oppression becomes the study of "oppressivities," while educational reforms become "educativities"—or equally faddish prefixes, with "intereducationality" joining the many terms that begin with bio-, cyber-, hetero-, homo-, or techno-. "Don't worry if you're not entirely sure what a term means," she writes reassuringly. "With the correct combination of prefixes and suffixes, you will most likely arrive at something that at least appears fashionable, if not profound." To these tics may be added the habit of pluralizing—a professor feels proudly subversive for having written "resurgences" with an *s*—which adds an aura of complexity to words even though we are well aware that by definition, they describe multiple situations.

"Academic writing is rotten." The author of this disillusioned but honest statement is himself a professor of psychology at Harvard. Steven Pinker, in an article coldly entitled "Why Academics Stink at Writing,"[17] finds in academic texts a wide variety of faults that would lead to their rejection by any editor who was not a complacent member of the academic milieu. His examples include metadiscourse (the tedious habit of inserting signposts such as "in the preceding paragraph, we have attempted to demonstrate X, in this paragraph, we will focus on the question of Y"); professional narcissism (summarizing everything you have been required to read in order to develop a thesis that is actually quite simple, but that you are unable to state in a single paragraph); an exaggerated view of how challenging an issue actually is (thinking about how children learn is viewed as abysmally difficult); the use of quotation marks for ordinary words ("learning" and "children"); hedging ("so to speak," "to some extent," "somewhat," "in part," "seemingly," "I would argue") to mark a subjective distance from a statement that you are not quite willing to stand behind; metaconceptualization ("approaching this subject from a law-enforcement perspective" instead of "calling the police," or using a "prejudice-reduction model" instead of "reducing prejudice"), which makes the slightest activity or reality the equivalent of a concept. Finally, Pinker mentions the writer's inability to guide the reader by presenting an argument step by step.

In criticizing his peers, Pinker challenges the common belief that all scientific discourse is an opaque insiders' affair. He also rejects the traditional accusation that scholars deliberately make their language opaque so that no one will understand them. While this suspicion may be justified in some cases, for Pinker, other, more important factors are involved. One of these is the fact that scholars are locked into the institutional economy and the hallowed concept of peer-reviewed scientific work, leading them to develop a form of writing whose goal is not communication or exchange, but a self-presentation that conforms with their environment. To this we might add the indifference, or even the contempt, that scholars as a professional group feel toward the public, even though the public funds most of their activities. Articles are often written, edited, printed, and distributed (chiefly to those who have contributed to them) to enable authors to add a line to their resumé. As time goes by, scholars cease to care about writing skills or readers, real or imagined: they become unable to imagine the thought processes of someone who is not immersed in their field of knowledge. The outcome is regressive. "A 3-year-old who sees a toy being hidden while a second child is out of the room assumes that the other child will look for it in its actual location rather than where she last saw it," as Pinker writes, illustrating the infantilized condition of many scholars who cannot imagine a state of awareness different from their own.

It is actually much more difficult to write clearly than to write opaquely. Nicolas Boileau wrote, "Whatever is well conceived is clearly said, and the words to say it flow with ease." Pinker is more negative: "When Calvin explained to Hobbes, 'With a little practice, writing can be an intimidating and impenetrable fog,' he got it backward. Fog comes easily to writers; it's the clarity that requires practice." Despite the fact that writing cannot be dissociated from thought, academics neglect it, so they end up misunderstanding their own profession. Some even feel contempt for critical works, written outside academia, that are addressed to both insiders and the public. Yet how many university professors can equal the skill of a writer like Naomi Klein in helping citizens increase their knowledge and deepen their thinking? An academic may look down on the writing of an investigative journalist such as Greg Palast, without reflecting on his own inability to produce anything as incisive and illuminating.

It is hardly surprising, then, that professors spend their time writing multimedia slideshows instead of books. What more can we expect from people who need so many technological crutches to move around? As Franck Frommer noted in his book *How PowerPoint Makes You Stupid: The Faulty Causality, Sloppy Logic, Decontextualized Data, and Seductive Showmanship That Have Taken Over Our Thinking*, computer slides do not simply accompany acts of communication, they transform them by making them ineffectual. As soon as you rely on this crutch, you are virtually obliged to base your teaching on clichés that never go beyond ideological buzzwords, using illustrations of strictly anecdotal value and bullet lists that reduce ideas to a brutal hierarchy of simplistic slogans. Finally, sentences themselves are disappearing from the university along with the logical connections, subtle relations, paradoxes, and nuances they allow. The diagrammatic quality of PowerPoint materials plunges the mind into a tangle of incomprehensible codes. What is the real meaning, for instance, of the boxes in which entire categories of actors are placed, or the arrows of an organizational chart that is supposed to illustrate institutional dynamics? Having observed the panic displayed at conferences by academics who depend on this software, we can only conclude that PowerPoint extinguishes the mind's autonomy.

Small intellectuals

In 1951 a Canadian professor of English, Marshall McLuhan, identified Clark Kent as a symbol of the twentieth-century academic. Superman's civilian double is the true hero of the story, which was originally imagined by two teenagers. The bumbling reporter seems to embody the foolish and clumsy intellectual of the time. Thinking of himself as a nobody, he is reduced to fantasies of greatness (expressed today as excellence and prestige). Whether he is a pathetic citizen or a caped superhero plunging into danger, America's infatuation for this character signals the loss of its relationship to structured thought. According to McLuhan's analysis in *The Mechanical Bride*, Superman embodies the abdication of the responsibility to think. In his heroic aspect, this abdication is shown by his unilateral character, the way he reduces justice to a simple matter of force, and his claim, without instruction or experience, to "flawless intelligence about all things." His impatience with "the laborious processes of civilized life" and his marked penchant for "violent solutions" are equally clear manifestations of his vanity. And as a failure in civilian life, he reflects "the psychological defeat of technological man."[18]

McLuhan defines this period as one in which research and teaching institutions were losing all self-respect. Through the participation of these institutions in "technological and specialist education"[19] driven first by the war economy, then by an industrial order that programmed the obsolescence of consumer goods to ensure their continuous renewal, intellectual life found itself in complete disarray. "Production for use? Yes. But for the briefest possible use consistent with the rigging of the market for the pyramiding of profits."[20] The research emerging from this process was so morally disinvested that in the end, the only thing that mattered to scientists was the scope of their research funding, their laboratory, and their institution. Their professional life—no longer a vocation—was strictly limited, rather like Clark Kent. And as McLuhan points out, "the smaller and meaner the man, the more he craves to possess . . . superhuman power." For McLuhan, "the key to Superman is Clark Kent the useless."[21]

While citizens, thinkers, and scientists were finding no reason to believe themselves any more than a cog in a vast machine, the machine itself was taking on a heroic aspect as it gathered into itself all of the labour power at its disposal. "Great physical and industrial power"[22] knows how to subject academics to its authority so that they will become its employees and work to increase its profits.

> Those who submit to [university] training only because it will link them more effectively to a great economic and bureaucratic mechanism are using their best years and faculties as a means of enslaving

themselves. They are seizing opportunities in order to have the economic means to be exactly like everybody else.[23]

Researchers who choose to stay within the confines of "pragmatism" are sentencing themselves to smallness. They see large-scale industry, the military, the state bureaucracy, and global financial institutions as superpowers to which they are subject, as "a multitude of powerless individuals, many of whom are deeply resentful of their condition."[24]

Superman is the image of a hero built on the basis of academic skills, but, as the Leviathan of an individualistic era, he makes academics small and contemptible. Unsurprisingly, then, this obscure object of desire was given prominence and verisimilitude through the efforts of university graduates. They applied their expertise and knowledge to aesthetic productions that made this emblem of the era's repressed suffering ever more fascinating. Capitalist production companies transformed the comic strip character into the hero of a radio epic; then came cartoons and pathetic television montages; rudimentary special effects were first attempted at the movies; finally, science created the feats of computer graphics that have been so popular in the twenty-first century. Technical knowledge has made the character's aesthetic more and more "real," as if the goal were to move from representation to presentation, from narrative to hallucination. The preview of a famous 1978 version already emphasized mediological advances ("the awesome technology of film") that suddenly made the character more plausible. In 2013, the same discourse prevailed: we mocked the old-fashioned use of pneumatics and superimposed images, while praising the technical exploits that now made Superman look utterly real. Suddenly the exploits were on a par with the superhero himself.

While graphic technicians play their part, others are also involved. Psychologists and neurologists monitor the effect of plots on viewers. Stories must be altered according to today's psychological and political climate in order to maintain the audience's illusions. Should Superman be tough or sensitive, fallible or invincible, resilient or prone to anger? Scientists work with focus groups, surveys, analyses, and theories to shape characters in the most appropriate way. Marie Bénilde has mercilessly dissected the role played by university research—in psychology, neurology, and semiology, not to mention computer science, engineering, marketing, and business management—in cajoling and manipulating our minds.[25] This has never been more true. With neuro-aesthetics, and especially the neurocinematics developed by psychologist Uri Hasson at Princeton University, storytelling no longer relies on "pity and terror," those old-fashioned elements that claimed cathartic power, to create viewer identification, but on an acute analysis of the medial prefrontal cortex—that part of the brain that lights up at the moment when subjects say to themselves "That's exactly me!" even as they look at very different scenes and stories. Focus groups are no longer surveys of what carefully selected viewers like or don't like. Instead, functional magnetic resonance imaging is used to study the responses of viewers' brains. Most of these studies are far from disinterested: the goal is to find out how to make brains look favourably on, and identify with, characters who are often deeply ideological. Specifically, university-trained technicians have helped develop the figure of a superhero iconically destined to redeem institutions; in this sense, they are depriving their own practice of high aims, while Hollywood firms are the major beneficiaries of their research.

Playing the game

It is genuinely sad to read so many harsh accounts of the pointless scientific work, the self-censorship that governs it, and the various abuses that are observed on campus. And as you become familiar with contemporary reports, books, and documents on academia, you can foresee that the institution will not protest. The university has gone through a vast and perverse transformation. The accuracy of this diagnosis is confirmed by the institution's inability to respond to its critics, including a number of courageous professors who speak from within the university.

Relationships within the university are so spectacularly noxious that sociologist Alexandre Afonso, who teaches in the political economy department of King's College in London and has studied drug trafficking structures, has no hesitation in comparing the university's organizational patterns with those of organized crime. His article "How Academia Resembles a Drug Gang," published in 2013 on the website of the London School of Economics and Political Science, compares the highly unequal incomes found in trafficking networks—where street sellers earn a wretched "salary" and big bosses rake in the profits—with the compensation systems that prevail in the university. Afonso wondered why small dealers were willing to work for a rate that was sometimes lower than the minimum wage. The answer, he says, is that "the prospect of future wealth, rather than current income and working conditions, is the main driver for people to stay in the business: low-level drug sellers forgo current income for (uncertain) future wealth. . . . They're ready to 'get rich or die trying.'"[26]

This hope attracts enough candidates to ensure that there will always be someone to do the job. University managers, chair holders, and members of the professoriate, just like drug lords, do not feel any need to ensure that the wealth they receive is more fairly distributed. Speaking of "dualisation," Afonso compares the system to a fortress: those who manage to get inside enjoy full benefits, leaving others with only the hope of being able to join them. While they wait, both small drug dealers and university graduates who have been left by the wayside may earn as little as nine hundred dollars a month. For precarious excluded scholars, small contracts alternate with frightening periods of emptiness, at a crucial point in their lives when they would surely prefer to advance their research and raise a family.

According to Marie-Ève Maillé, who holds a doctorate in communications, graduate students are instrumentalized by professors who need to outsource their excess work for low pay.

> University professors already work too much, and they are constantly required to do more. It follows that they need PhD students to write a large proportion of the scholarly articles they must produce every year, as if this knowledge could be produced at the same rate as low-grade sausages. Professors also need PhD students to teach many of the courses that they can no longer give because they are too busy attending department meetings, faculty committee meetings, and the many other meetings that clutter up their agenda. And professors need PhD students to write long sections of the grant proposals that they keep on producing like compulsive gamblers sitting in front of a video lottery terminal: as soon as their funding comes in, they have to start pursuing the next grant. Under this system, it is not clear when they have time to spend all the money they get.[27]

The academic world tends to produce resentment in PhD students. To avoid this pitfall, Tiphaine Rivière, a graduate student who failed to submit her thesis, wrote a caustic graphic novel[28] that describes the many abusive aspects of university life. She highlights deadly internal struggles between professors who use students as proxies, intellectual relationships with professors based on rhetorical equivocation, minor courses taught on a volunteer basis, and badly paid administrative work. There are romantic breakups, isolation, a great deal of egotism, and frequent depression.

Of course, the fact that there are so many people with PhDs in Western countries—an increasing number—may explain why some of them are unemployed. But objective labour market conditions have also changed over the years. In Germany, according to Afonso, few programs or structures enable scholars who have just obtained their PhD to work.

In the United States, "more than 40% of teaching staff at universities are now part-time faculty without tenure, or adjunct lecturers paid per course given, with no health insurance or the kind of other things associated with a standard employment relationship."[29] In Canada, there are three times as many PhD holders as there are permanent teaching positions to be filled in universities. According to a French government source, the rate of unemployment is much higher among French PhD holders than among those who have a master's degree, and among PhD holders who do find work, 32 per cent are in jobs that do not call on their research skills.[30] Today's emphasis on getting grants and publishing prestigious work leads university administrators and faculty to minimize the value of teaching and to assign such work to underpaid staff.

In drawing a series of analogies between the university and the mafia, Afonso could also have mentioned the rhetoric of the "game" that prevails in both environments. While "playing the game" is a common phrase within academia, "the game" is a practically mythical reference in the criminal world. *The Wire*, a TV series intended as a sociological fiction on drug trafficking and its repression, presents a study of the inexhaustible and problematic meanings of an organization based on the idea of the game. Within the rigorously hierarchical circles of both drug traffickers and formal institutions (political parties, police forces, the media, and the academic world), the game imposes its blind law and its cowardly intuitions. To think of relationships with the world in this way requires an abdication of the mind. Playing the game involves too many contradictory meanings to allow for escape from the arbitrary reality of naked power relations and shameful underhanded dealings. And yet the expression "playing the game" conceals the true situation: these three simple words make things look harmless, playful, and even childlike.

The game would appear, in the first place, to be a set of unwritten rules and procedures that are informal but habitual, and that must be followed in a given environment in order to achieve your goals. Playing the game involves participating in rituals (being seen at an evening event, making a conspicuous donation to a certain charity, congratulating a colleague for an excellent article that you have not read), that, while not obligatory, indicate your loyalty to the group, the network, or the institution. But the hidden side of these social rites is a violent one. A lack of allegiance to the network will be punished by death, either symbolically or with real bullets. The unwritten rules are enforced by a ruthless authority. And because the rules are not always clear, the game itself is not clear; even establishing the rules of the game is a game, and the game, finally, is less a set of rules than a power dynamic established by actors attempting to impose their rules on others.

The game, in fact, is twofold. It looks like a sport, or a (latent) war, within a framework that provides no clarity. And in this game where there are basically no rules, anything goes. We already know that playing the game means moving away from the formal field: it may involve cheating, or acting with a crude immorality that can even include overt violence or crime. It is a given that some will be caught. Losing, however, does not put an end to the game. On the contrary, it is a part of it, like landing on "Go to jail"; incarceration or precarity are just everyday possibilities. If someone's scheming turns out to be fatal to us, then we will bite the dust trying to gain the grant or position that we legitimately deserve. "Yo, it's the game." The game includes hierarchies of rules, ranging from strictly conventional systems to outright hostility. There may be a set of conventions related to loyalty, a set of punitive measures to deal with lapses, and random eviction when you are knocked over by an antagonistic order that imposes a new set of rules for the game as a whole. More crudely, the game involves pure authority unleashed within a competitive order that is embodied in both capitalism and the power of the mafia. Both may cultivate systems involving laws and codes of honour, but they do it for the purpose of mystification.

Actually, playing in the sense of following the rules is only for the weak. For those who are able to think big, the game means surveying the entire situation from above in order to dominate it by arbitrarily determining its rules. As literature professor Paul Allen Anderson of the University of

Michigan says in an article on *The Wire*, it means "to stay ahead in the game by asserting interpretive authority over it."[31] For those who dominate it, the game is fiercely competitive: a power struggle relying on arbitrary means determines who can make others play by establishing a semi-institutionalized power dynamic in a territory, or field of influence, where they impose their unwritten law. Varlam Shalamov, who knows what he is talking about, says that you can't improvise your way to the top of the game; mastery is something that has to be achieved. In *Sketches of the Criminal World*, he writes:

> It's not enough just to steal, you have to belong to the "order" [of hereditary con men], and this is achieved not just through thievery or murder. Certainly not every "heavyweight," certainly not every murderer, is accorded a place of honour among con men just because he happens to be a robber or a murderer. They have their own "guardians" of moral purity, as well as their most important "trade secrets," by which are worked out ... the general laws of this world (which, like life itself, are subject to change).[32]

The game is a euphemism for another political order: one that is badly structured, that cannot be spoken of even by those who maintain it year in and year out, and that is arbitrary, unpredictable, and, of course, resolutely antidemocratic. Democracy would mean being able to deliberate together on the rules, their justification, and how strictly they should be applied. Our model, the master con man, first positions himself in relation to a psychotic law-making system that belongs to him alone: it is based on the power dynamic that he is able to establish. Formal rules—laws, regulations, protocols—may continue to exist, of course, but they are destined to be either broken or instrumentalized. In any case, powerful agents are in a position where they can oversee the game. They, who establish the dynamics of the game, may use formal laws to defeat an adversary, to discredit an idea, or to crush a popular movement. Anyone who says to himself, "I'm not living the way you do, I have my own life with other laws, other interests, another definition of honour" is, in his own way, a master con man. According to Shalamov, the "ethics" that derive from this way of life involve abusing others according to a philosophy of debasement.

For those who are subject to it, the game basically consists of lubricating their relationships with those who arbitrarily establish the game. Having entered a bewildering maze of rules, they try not to stand out in any way to avoid the penalties their peers or authorities will inflict. At best, they will attempt to stay afloat, earn their place, and keep to it in circumstances over which they have no control, always complying with expectations as they understand them. Playing the game means to re-establish it in your own way, claim a part of it for yourself, consolidate what you believe to be its rules, and score points by finding others to abuse or to deceive. Mediocre people keep asking for more; they like to show that no one can make a fool of them, and they will do anything to avoid getting thrown out of the game. These are the powerful minds that "get it." Of course, their strategic and sometimes belligerent approach removes from the game any possibility of disinterested thought. Their domination leads inevitably to the social death of thought.

Where do we end up when we apply "liberal" (meaning market) principles to areas where they are irrelevant? Step by step, university administrators adopt ways of doing things that lead them to operations either verging on the illegal or entirely illicit. In response to a number of scandals in Quebec that exposed the illegal funding of political institutions by criminal organizations in the construction industry, Michel Seymour, professor of philosophy at the Université de Montréal, has been monitoring developments, tirelessly reminding us that most of the research investments carried out by universities and the Quebec government over the past few years have involved real estate.[33] The projects include two university hospitals, the projected Université de Montréal campus on a former railway shunting yard in the Outremont borough, the disastrous

Îlot Voyageur real estate project launched by the Université du Québec à Montréal, and a high-rise that the same university would like to build near Montreal's Quartier des Spectacles. We can add to this list buildings erected by universities outside their natural territory, such as the Université de Sherbrooke campus on Montreal's south shore or the Université de Rimouski campus across the river from Quebec City, as part of a pointless competition between institutions for the same group of potential students. We might also mention the mind-boggling sums that administrators of various universities choose to pay themselves: in March 2012, Radio-Canada estimated that heads of Quebec universities were receiving over half a million dollars a year in salaries and benefits, while in countries like France, they are generally paid somewhere between 60,000 and 150,000 euros. North American university presidents seem convinced that the extreme standards practised by the boards of multinational corporations should apply to them as well.

There are also spectacular failures involving some of the world's most controversial tax havens. Problems can easily arise when universities are guided by their trusted alumni. Université de Montréal administrators caused the university's pension plan (RRUM), belonging to its ten thousand employees, to lose a hundred million dollars when they entrusted this amount to a manager from the British Virgin Islands. Germain Bourgeois, who was responsible for the university's investments from 1998 to 2000, on five different occasions invested the pension plan's money in a British Virgin Islands hedge fund managed by the Lancer Group—a group also established in Delaware, a US state operating as a tax haven. The hedge fund manager, Michael Lauer, persisted in overestimating the value of investments until the entire amount disappeared. The university was not the only sucker in this affair. The City of Laval was also taken in, as were private corporations:

> Documents show that Bombardier, the Lucie and André Chagnon Foundation, Desjardins, the National Bank, and the École polytech-

nique were also persuaded to invest in this fund; apparently, they all took the advice of Germain Bourgeois. In all, Quebec investments entrusted to Lauer appear to total over half a billion dollars.[34]

All of this money has disappeared. The dealings of the Lancer Group have been investigated by the US Securities and Exchange Commission (SEC), the agency that regulates the American stock market. The company was eventually required to pay a $62 million fine, without, however, being formally charged with fraud.

As for the British Virgin Islands, it is a favoured location for financial piracy, as the university would know if it educated people to criticize tax havens instead of using them. According to the Financial Secrecy Index established by the international Tax Justice Network to assess the lack of accountability in various legislation, the British Virgin Islands is an ultra-permissive regime where bank secrecy and the lack of substantial legislation provides cover for any fraudster choosing to register there. The International Monetary Fund says that a very large number of corporations have amassed $615 billion in this small archipelago; ultimately, however, we cannot know whether this figure truly reflects the amount of money concentrated in these islands. According to the Tax Justice Network, the British Virgin Islands is one of the most harmful jurisdictions in the world. *Le Monde* reports that this hideout, formerly the haunt of Slobodan Milošević's Serbian friends, is used by Chinese real estate investors such as Deng Jiagui, brother-in-law of President Xi Jinping, to move illicit funds.[35] French wine grower Dominique Giroud also used an offshore entity located in the British Virgin Islands, which led him to be accused in Switzerland in 2012 "of having concealed 13 million francs from tax authorities thanks to complex financial manoeuvres involving a firm from the city of Zoug and another firm located offshore in the British Virgin Islands."[36] A British subsidiary of Sonatrach, Algeria's national oil company, owes British tax authorities $45 million that it has deposited in this highly accommodating jurisdiction.[37]

One of the most spectacular bankruptcies in history, the turn-of-the-century Parmalat affair, also leads us back to the British Virgin Islands, one of the tax havens Parmalat used. In other words, the Université de Montréal has been in a position to know since the 1980s, if not earlier, that the British Virgin Islands' libertarian regime was in no way a safe place to put money. Why then did the university administration choose to invest colossal amounts there—amounts representing up to 10 per cent of its employees' pension plan? Why did Montreal's École polytechnique do the same thing? What was the university doing at this time? It was boasting of "exceptional returns," as evidenced by a 1998 article from its internal publication, *Forum.* "The RRUM fund is benefiting from exceptional returns, ranking first in the category of pension funds worth $250 million and more." Fortunately, "members of the pension fund who feel jittery when they contemplate stock market upheavals need not be concerned. The RRUM fund continues to be in excellent financial health, not only for 1997, but also for the first nine months of 1998."[38] And the last shall be first. The affair was known within the Université de Montréal by 2003, as revealed in January 2004 by a Radio-Canada television program, *Zone libre.*[39] A class-action suit filed by professors was unfortunately settled out of court, leaving a number of questions unanswered: For what purpose are university funds managed? And what game are administrators playing?

Of course, Quebec universities are not alone in putting their money in tax havens. In the fall of 2017, the Paradise Papers revealed that major North American and British universities are now deeply committed to offshore investment strategies. Oxford, Cambridge, and Oxbridge colleges "have secretly invested tens of millions of pounds in offshore funds, including in a joint venture to develop oil exploration and deep-sea drilling," while over a hundred US universities and colleges—including Princeton, Columbia, and Stanford—have invested funds in offshore entities. The University of Toronto's endowment and pension funds have

money in two offshore tax havens. These investments are often characterized by extreme secrecy: according to Yale University scholar Norman
Silber, even board members may be kept in the dark.[40]

The discipline of economics, as taught by the university to those who
will eventually manage the institution, is not likely to prevent this kind of
problem. In courses most often dedicated to teaching ideology, one of the
myths conveyed with a kind of frenzied yearning is that of a market involving rational actors who, to the best of their knowledge and ability, make
decisions according to specific contexts. How many intelligent students
who want to understand the reasons for the world's dysfunctional financial
and industrial evolution have discovered that attending schools of business,
law, or political science actually makes them feel more ignorant than before
they were admitted? The academic institution both relays and produces a
discourse of ignorance.

Losers

If by chance academics fail to grasp the necessity of rational reserve, balance, and abstruseness, brutal means will be employed to make sure that
they get it. Scholars whose work displeases powerful interests will pay
for it: they will be harassed, laid off, or unable to get a job. Sixteen North
American academics have described this situation in *Academic Freedom in
Conflict*,[41] a collection of articles focusing on the restrictive standards and
official regulations that govern, and sometimes suffocate, critical or novel
points of view within academe. It could also have highlighted the policies
of "competition" and "excellence" that subject university programs to
business requirements. The university shaped by these forces can legitimately be described as unrecognizable, or perhaps morally bankrupt.

The disappointment experienced by those who have played the game
and demonstrated their trust in the regime—those whom the con men

describe as the suckers, to use Shalamov's expression—can be extreme. "My diploma hurts," said Catherine Martellini in 2014 as she came to realize that in proffering slogans like "the knowledge economy," the university is misleading students with empty words.[42] Not only does the university harm students' research vocation through excessive professionalization and instrumentalization, but it also does so to no purpose. Why does it spend years training graduates and then fling them out into the wilderness, knowing full well that it is unable to provide careers for over 70 per cent of them? Martellini offers a devastating example: a state-funded institution keeps on training scores of librarians, while state-decided budget cuts inevitably lead to major layoffs in this area. Although it is obsessed with the issue of graduate employability, the university does not seem to care about making the general public understand the nature of any discipline other than engineering, administration, medicine, psychology, law, and a few others. The society that funds the university is not given a clear explanation of why literary studies, urban planning, or sociology are relevant to its own life and development, probably because scholars themselves no longer have time to consider this question. In the long run, this makes academics and especially PhD holders look hopelessly marginal, yet if the university were dedicated to openly sharing and developing thought, their skills would be highly valued both professionally and from a citizen's perspective.

Playing the game is therefore very costly, whether you participate blindly or are forced willy-nilly to comply with its unwritten rules. Requirements now include excessive publishing beyond anyone's normal abilities, to the point where the whole thing becomes excruciating (one option is to recycle articles or share signatures with others to increase your numbers). You must also find money by any means possible, even if this threatens the independence of your research—which may happen, since you will need to seduce both the community of your (conformist) peers and ideological funding bodies. Participants eventually become travesties of themselves: as they fully commit to their role as government consultants and ideologues, or sell themselves to corporate masters, their academic personas become increasingly hollow. For instance, documents obtained by Greenpeace show that Wei-Hock Soon, a scientist at the Harvard-Smithsonian Center for Astrophysics, was paid by the oil industry to claim that variations in the sun's energy can largely explain recent global warming. Dr. Soon was often seen on news programs, at conferences, or testifying before Congress and in US state capitals.[43] James Cresswell, an expert in flowers and bees at the University of Exeter in England, was paid by pesticide giant Syngenta to produce work showing that the death of bee colonies throughout the world was not related to pesticides,[44] and Coca-Cola has funded scientific studies claiming that obesity is caused not by calories but by lack of exercise.[45] Professors at medical schools funded by pharmaceutical companies have been known to minimize the side effects of drugs when discussing them in the classroom.[46] And in 2010, the documentary *Inside Job* showed that many economists teaching in universities, publishing "scientific" articles and providing advice as members of institutional committees, were also on the boards of major financial or industrial corporations, the most revealing example being the dean of the Columbia Business School, Glenn Hubbard.[47]

Luc Bonneville, communication professor at the University of Ottawa, published an article in 2014 based on a series of interviews dealing with the increased psychological pressure experienced by academics. Under the heading "Playing the Game of Performance," he writes:

> This basic "rule of the game" means that pressure first develops in relation to one's own scientific "production," since professors "know" that they must publish no matter what. When they do not publish enough, some develop feelings of embarrassment, or even guilt. . . . For it is always possible to publish more. One can always be more productive and one is always being compared to someone more productive than oneself. Therefore, one must apply for grants at every opportunity, in order to remain part of the research world.[48]

The article includes fascinating statements such as the following, from an established professor of history:

> The pressure on my younger colleagues to apply for research grants is very, very high. . . . When I started [in the late 1980s], I was expected to be a good teacher and to publish my thesis as a book or a series of articles. There were no requirements. I was not encouraged, nor was there any pressure to apply for funding. But my young colleagues are now in the game of [applying for] funding.[49]

Many denounce these working conditions, but few, according to this study, seem to believe they could accomplish anything by stepping outside the current academic game—as if nothing else were possible, even though professors are one of the few socio-professional categories that do not answer to a boss. They play the game and become "entrepreneurs" in a sovereign manner. No one speaks of the damage this conformism inflicts on their work, which necessarily becomes mediocre. No one acknowledges what Yvon Rivard pointed out in 2012:

> A "good" professor today is one who is exempt from teaching because he has obtained so many grants that he must devote himself to researching something that he already knows, as a project submitted (along with a budget and bibliography) to scholars whom he has assessed in previous competitions.[50]

On the contrary, while continuing to describe themselves as overwhelmed and exhausted, academics coyly maintain the confusion between proliferative article publishing and "research," even though it is well understood today that the one actually harms the other, and that recycling content and having many people sign articles written by a single person are common practices. They even measure their feelings of "not doing enough," not being sufficiently "productive," or not "excelling," in quantitative terms: "If I were in the bottom third [consisting of the lowest performers among professors], I wouldn't like it. I would put pressure on myself to join the top third," says one whose life is defined by her peers— those who blindly participate, like her, in the same system.

Taking a more analytical approach, law professor Andrée Lajoie finds that these feelings of guilt are caused by the conditions of research grants: the issue is structural before becoming psychological. In her book *Vive la recherche libre!*, she says that scholars have been subject, since the end of the 1990s, to programs that, for instance, "favour partnerships between researchers and people involved in practice, intervention, or policy development (thus implying concertation)" and that involve greater "emphasis on teamwork." One consequence of encouraging such research networks is to neutralize initiative and accentuate intellectual conformism, strategic alliances, and complicit interests to the detriment of "free research."[51] Lajoie notes that when there is an obligation to assign research tasks to teams, there is generally also support for undertakings that are thematically "targeted"; a utilitarian approach of this kind is suited to the needs of the various institutionalized powers. In this way, conformism is institutionalized according to perverse dynamics that bring more and more researchers first to compare themselves to others using a single set of criteria, and then to compete while believing that the pressure comes from within themselves. In France, the ethics committee of the National Centre for Scientific Research (CNRS) estimated, in a document published in May 2014, that subjecting university research to the criteria of private enterprise was harmful to its development. According to the committee, "in practice, the predominant use of criteria of excellence as a basis for a research policy involves both risk and bias." This is because, among other things, "posting scientific priorities may have a negative effect on researchers' creativity," and "competition that is too strong leads to distortion and loss of efficiency."[52]

Unlike Lajoie, the CNRS ethicists believe that rules based on the individual lead to the development of useless research projects. For this reason, the authors recommend that the institution "provide enough basic support and human resources to sustain quality teams that would not be subject to the 'excellence' criteria as posted." The committee deplores that "the call-for-tenders system too often leads to a quest for themes that must always be new, and that are related to fads rather than the exploitation of resources," and that it "rather naturally fosters the development of individualistic behaviour," even though "high-level achievements are rarely produced by a single individual, but are usually the outcome of collective work."[53] However you approach this institutionalized phenomenon, the general conclusion is the same.

These criticisms eventually lead to an understandable apathy among those who are dedicated to the craft of teaching. Writers invited to contribute to an issue of *Contre-jour* on imagination and teaching tried to fall back on positions that would still enable them to endow the classroom with a powerful meaning—as a place where you still can be astonished "by a flow of words that leaves you motionless as you concentrate," the last place where stupidity is not tolerated, the place where you can find emancipation through a paradoxical relationship to rules, or the place that provides the first intimate memories of a crude and powerful love that you will cultivate much later.[54] Many of these writers struggled through labyrinths of disillusionment to reach these positions. Wise or resigned, they clearly found it difficult to rise above the disillusioned critique of university reality. From the last islands of non-corrupt teaching, it seems as if no horizon can be imagined.

Perverse effects

A French PhD student enrolled in a Quebec university uses the image of an abusive partner in a relationship to describe the thousand and one manipulative tactics the university employs. As part of your relationship of seduction and fusion with the institution, everything is done gradually to ensure your dependency. It starts with love at first sight (you are the best, our future together will be extraordinary); then, the university introduces rules that it alone understands. "Time goes by and you spend so much time specializing in a very narrow field that you have come to think that academia/research is not only *one* growth opportunity for you but THE ONLY way to develop your full potential professionally."[55] Having become a captive, you cannot escape a series of steps that are part of the program and that often turn out to be either sterile rituals of humiliation, or blackmail associated with starvation-level funding or purely symbolic forms of status: "You must explain in long letters why you're asking to take one more year to finish your dissertation and beg the department for the authorization." These repeated blows are characteristic of the period of "loss of self-esteem." This is also when you first notice the obvious irregularities and arbitrary nature of hiring processes, as well as the sometimes fatal wounds they can inflict.

At this stage, pushed to the brink and sometimes disgusted with yourself or even with the realms of knowledge and beauty for which you have made so many sacrifices, you begin to see any offer as a favour, whether it is teaching a course for poverty-level wages or acting as a volunteer facilitator for a symposium. "A bouquet of flowers and the promise that it will all change, promise," continues the author, sustaining her metaphor.

And since you love teaching/doing research (*you love him/her*), since the outside world is frightening (*you're isolated*), and since you are convinced that no one will ever hire someone as specialized as yourself (*anyways, I'm such a loser, no one else will ever love me*), you keep on hoping that you will one day get hired (*that your partner will change, and will treat you as you deserve*), and leave to slowly die out (until next time) your vague desire to retrain.

This type of relationship may not always be a metaphor. Literature professor Yvon Rivard describes both the virtues of teaching and how perverted it may become. The vocation that he wants to defend and illustrate—as a reader of Virginia Woolf, Hermann Broch, George Steiner, or Pierre Vadeboncœur—involves presenting students with texts that are worthy of being taught as an entry into wider issues. These are issues greater than oneself, so great, in fact, that a teacher who is not jaded lives, independently of her professional contract and required tasks, for her own need to share with a classroom the unsettlement they evoke in her. "You become a professor, as you become a writer, because you have an ability to receive shocks and an inability to stand them without explaining them to yourself through writing or teaching."[56] A great text embodies something that exceeds prefabricated representations as well as acquired forms of understanding. The goal of teaching is to reconcile the student with that part of herself that is able to grasp fundamental questions, or aesthetic positions, that are profoundly unsettling. It also involves accompanying the other part of the student—the part of her that finds it difficult to sustain the impact of the text and to translate the meaning of its fullness into formal terms. In this, Rivard is in agreement with French philosopher Patrice Loraux, who argues that a teacher must traumatize students to some degree, however minimal, in order to provoke in them an imperative reflection.[57] Epistemologist Dominique Pestre says that astonishment when you encounter the grandeur of objects is also experienced in disciplines that are erroneously viewed as colder and more level-headed, such as physics.[58] From this starting point, Rivard develops a subtle reflection on death, arguing that knowledge insistently asks us to develop a kind of ease that will allow us to look at death and possibly accept it as inevitable. This means that our attempts to know, and to teach, call for a humble relationship with knowledge.

As part of the seductive relationship that is at the heart of the teaching process, professors sometimes abuse their power to the point where they cause distress that may even lead to suicide. Refuting the idea that these are simply isolated cases, sites such as Academia Is Killing My Friends or Depressed Academics collect the stories of members of the academic community who are harmed by the institution's stifling and oppressive ambiance. Moral and psychological harassment, sexual aggression, discrimination: all are present as part of relations in which students often have very little power, especially if they belong to more vulnerable groups (women, international students, visible minorities, and so on). Rivard's book focuses on the ethical issue of sexual transgression between a male professor and a female student, quoting situations from the novels of J.M. Coetzee, Peter Handke, and Philip Roth and challenging the ideas of essayist Jean Larose, who has developed a theory asserting the legitimacy of such actions. These transgressions prevent the student from following the lines of flight opened by the text that would lead her to knowledge, while the professor standing between the student and the text gains a contemptible satisfaction. Rivard compares these failings to a young man's inability to learn how to be a father by sublimating his immediate desires through rites that have been used in human societies over very long periods.

Violence is at its peak in American universities, where excellence in sports and a "work hard, play hard" ethos can take priority over intellectual considerations. American universities have progressively become philistine schools where misogyny, racism, and alcoholism are openly cultivated, to the point of raising concern in the student community and among faculty administrators and residents of university towns. For financial reasons, universities must attract athletes who are destined for a professional career, which is why they spare no effort in emphasizing the "sexy" and "fun" character of campus life. This kind of marketing, and the indulgence of administrations, are responsible—even more than the individual athletes involved—for the depraved mores that lead to such a prevalence of rape that some now speak of an epidemic in American universities. According to the *Journal of Adolescent Health*, nearly 18 per cent of the women enrolled in universities are victims of rape or attempted rape during their first year.[59] This phenomenon, as well as a long tradition of racist incidents, has had a significant effect on the development of a discourse that opposes them: political correctness treats elementary moral tenets as science, and obsessively analyzes social and political phenomena solely according to considerations relating to class, gender, and racialized groups.

Finding hope: Unemployed writers, precarious instructors, ignorant masters

When Swiss writer Denis de Rougemont lost his job in 1933 and settled into a borrowed house on the island of Ré, he described himself as *en chômage*, "in unemployment" as an active state, rather than *au chômage*, simply unemployed.[60] When thinking is your vocation, even being unemployed is work. Rougemont, who was a professor of literature, describes this experience in a journal originally published in 1945. To begin with, he expresses surprise that the description of some intellectuals as "unemployed," in relation to others for whom thinking is a paid job, bears no relation to intellectual activity as such, that is, the activity of publishing and explaining ideas. An intellectual is seen as unemployed when he is not able to find another "regular job that sustains his budget," but such a job is marginal to his research activity; the activity of thinking is free and disinterested. "Most of the time, the intellectual does not need anything but paper and ink. Therefore, he will never be unemployed in an absolute sense, since he is always thinking, which is his job." He is one of the lucky few who escape unemployment as an essential "condition" that deeply undermines the person subject to it. For the intellectual, unemployment is a precarious status that has little to do with his capacity to work. When he is "in unemployment," his commitment can be greater than when he is confined by the schedule, standards, and objective expectations of a job. "When I stopped writing because I was tired, I did not experience the clear conscience of an employee who has done a day's work and can now think of something else."

Of course, precariousness makes it more difficult for a thinker to concentrate. As we follow Rougemont over two years, from the island of Ré to a Paris suburb and then to the Gard region of southern France, we see him plunge, not without anxiety, into laborious account keeping, trying to support himself and his partner through poorly paid lectures, last-minute translations, and freelance articles that strike him as more and more absurd. Providence intervenes, offering an unexpected scholarly prize. While his financial situation is difficult, the young Rougemont also finds it stimulating. He is forced to shift the focus of his attention, adjust his thought to realities unknown to the world of bourgeois knowledge, and carry out fruitful incursions into social and geographical environments left unexplored by others at the time.

Rougemont was no longer dealing with the people solely as an idea in the writings of Nikolai Berdyaev, which he edited, but also in his necessary relationships with the residents of the Gard or the island of Ré. This was a shock: he found that "the people," as described in humanistic writings and emancipatory manifestos, had little to do with "the people" that he met on an empirical basis. After a public event held in his village, he wrote: "It seems to me that this teaches me more about 'the people' than all of my previous experiences. In fact, it seems to me that it causes me to see 'the people' for the first time in my life." "The people" that he dealt with on a daily basis was a group that did not seem to have any idea of the intense thinking of which it was the object at the time, whether in bourgeois academic work or official Communist Party publications.

For non-intellectuals, the intellectual who drops by the village for a lecture is at most a fancy talker, whether or not what he says has any direct relation to tangible elements of their lives. Rougemont notes that few people understand the work that he does. When they visit him, they are more impressed by his typewriter than by the texts it might produce. His exile as an unemployed thinker helps him see the arbitrary nature of conventions regarding thought that intellectuals artificially maintain within their professional habitus. "There is probably a fatality internal to our culture: it enchants itself, criticizes itself, and legitimates itself. It has its own laws, sufficient unto themselves. Concepts combine according to affinities or repulsions that are not actually present in the facts or beings they are supposed to represent." Humbly, Rougemont develops a self-criticism of the desire for recognition expressed by thinkers who contribute nothing to public life, and have "little to give to those who are hungry for solid, elementary sustenance." He wonders: "What is the relation between the man with whom I am speaking and the word 'man' in my writing?" Once he is "far from Paris," the discrepancy he notices between the intellectual representation of the people and his actual relationship with the people is a kind of sociological shock, leading him to completely rethink his position. "One can leave behind the cities where 'careers' are made without leaving a real life behind," he writes, rediscovering the virtue of a writing capable of "being useful with grandeur."

Today's equivalent for Rougemont's unemployed writer might be a precarious contract teacher at a university. These teachers, sometimes known by terms reflecting their lowly status such as "sessionals" or "adjuncts," are the ones who experience anxiety because they are penniless or do not know if they will have a contract next term. Professors look down their noses at them, while claiming to be jealous of how "lucky" they are—for since they are only on contract, clearly they must have "time to write." Contract teachers are the university's proletarians, structurally free of the institution's main distortions. They are not required to find clients who will determine how departments are managed, to sit on committees, to network globally at academic conferences, to organize special issues of periodicals on a given theme in order to reach the promised land of excellence, or to produce as the machine requires. They are simply asked to do what the professor's vocation calls on them to do: teach. And unless they are completely incompetent, precarious university lecturers who teach, and who may even be active in environments other than the university, will be led to ask questions about the material they are transmitting, will make progress within themselves, and may—who knows?—develop original ideas at a reasonable pace.

Paradoxically, though, their presence is seen as symptomatic of bad teaching. In his book *The University in Ruins*, the late Bill Readings, who taught comparative literature, presented the increase in the number of teachers hired on "short-term or part-time contracts" as evidence of the university's failure. But while it is true that "the professariat is being proletarianized,"[61] paradoxically, the presence of contract teachers may be the university's only chance to escape the corruption that afflicts it, according to Readings's own assessment: its neglect of teaching, reliance on economic criteria to define research directions, frenzied networking, carefully designed career plans, and so on. These constraints have far less impact on precarious contract teachers. It goes without saying that such teachers are not by definition better people or better intellectuals than professors, but they are in an institutional position to avoid the pressure experienced by their professor peers and, therefore, to provide the institution with greater meaning through their practice both inside and outside the institution.

In a similar vein, philosopher Jacques Rancière states that he is not particularly indebted to his scientific training for the questions he has developed throughout his intellectual life. This is what emerges from the interviews he gave to Laurent Jeanpierre and Dork Zabunyan in a book called *The Method of Equality*.[62] As a student in preparatory classes for the entrance competition of France's prestigious École normale supérieure (ENS), Rancière observed "a fairly amazing number of bad teachers" and concluded that "the pinnacle of the teaching hierarchy had nothing to do with any level of competence or ability to teach."[63] On the contrary, exams and competitions were a set of rituals that produced an elite on the basis of a "precise gymnastic exercise"[64] (which in the late 1950s included mastery of Greek particles), far more than on the basis of humanist culture. Rancière explains that for this reason he assigned little value to teaching programs at the Sorbonne or ENS, preferring to open himself to masters—whom he would later challenge to some degree—such as Louis Althusser and Michel Foucault. But in any case, the figure of the master was being deconstructed.

> Basically, anything that provokes us is a master, as is possibly anything that whispers answers to you in relation to the provocation. This twin function of provoking you and whispering the answers to you works through a host of texts that might go from children's prayers to Kant and Hegel, and it also works through all sorts of encounters offered by people as much as by texts.[65]

This openness to many encounters led Rancière to recognize the multiplicity of the positions from which thought may be uttered. A prisoner who has thought about the world of the prison develops a theory about it, just as much as a sociologist mandated by the institution to carry out this task. The same is true of the intellectual production of workers, whose thought, whatever it may potentially lack, is already in action: it is not a "symbol of," an "expression of," and so on, that would require "translation" by an expert. Rancière's position is consistent: an internationally recognized thinker may have taken very few courses in his field, may deny the relevance of the competitions that gave him his status in the institutional hierarchy, and may develop his thinking by rejecting the canonical methods of his field. But to escape the resignation associated with the "critical" posture (one that is too often content with deciphering systemic failures without going any further), Rancière became interested in the spoken and written utterances of social actors who lacked the status of expert, property owner, or member of the ruling class.

Proletarian Nights was the first book in which he investigated the meaning of poems, letters, and other writings produced by workers. Breathing life into the theme of democracy, he later developed in *Disagreement* and *Hatred of Democracy* a definition related not to a formal regime but to a principle: intelligence is shared by all, and, in a system based on the premise of equality between subjects, we are all equally endowed with intelligence and will, which are the qualities required in order to govern. What Rancière describes in *The Method of Equality* is not a fantasy of identical equivalence between all; rather, he discusses what he calls a "non-specific competence"[66] in relation to politics. This means that there is no absolute science, no determined form of intelligence that might be identified once and for all to ensure the relevance of political decisions, such as the decision to send an army to a given territory or to give big business even more public funds. These are choices to which no science can give a definite basis. Politics exists when subjects engage in composing, recomposing, and thinking about what they have in common. The "sharing" at the heart of the political process involves both a shared location in thought and in space, and a way of analyzing this location, to the extent that the analysis can be debated by all. Here again, equality does not imply strict equivalency between subjects, but the fact "that although it is distributed differently, intelligence is the same for everyone. We can always encounter or construct situations where we can verify the equality of intelligence."[67] Thus, Rancière argues that drawing lots is the best way to designate who will govern in a democracy, since the ability to think does not belong exclusively to any one privileged social group, and since no hierarchical structure can be established on a given foundation once and for all. While drawing lots does not guarantee competence, there is no reason to believe that a randomly chosen assembly is less capable than an assembly created by the electoral process, since the latter process favours only one kind of knowledge: the knowledge of how to gain power.

Drawing lots to designate members of senates and upper chambers, in states subject to the rule of law, would be a transitional stage. It would not radically change the tradition of political debate surrounding partisan activities, but it would mean that to enact any law, elected officials would have to convince an assembly made up of ordinary people. Within this body representing the community's ability to debate the justification for proposed laws, "people," as they are vaguely designated by Rancière, would have the power to reverse a government's decision and would therefore develop a specific interest in public affairs. Instead of abandoning public affairs to worthies and strategists attracted by the struggle between politicians, people would, on the contrary, be aware of their ability to mobilize at any time to support or oppose a bill. This would also solve the problem of justification by election, that is, the fact that governments believe that winning an election is the equivalent of being given a blank cheque. However, Western "democracies" do not provide a place where such transformations might be discussed in a serious and sustained way.

Taking another road, psychoanalyst Jean-Pierre Winter argues for a view of teaching that is also based on autonomy. Unlike today's ideologues, in a recent essay[68] he humbly focuses on the "enigma of the circulation of knowledge" between generations, refusing to see how students acquire knowledge only in terms of pedagogical inculcation. It is clear that the power of knowing operates in every mind since childhood, as noted by Freud ("The little human being is frequently a finished product in his fourth or fifth year, and only reveals gradually in later years what has long been ready within him"[69]), Nietzsche ("The parents are always brought up by the children"[70]), the Talmud (which compares the embryo to a folded writing tablet[71]), and Thomas Aquinas, who believed that one person's teaching cannot produce science in another ("The disciple does not acquire fresh knowledge from his master, but is roused by him to consider what he knows"[72]). For Winter, as for Rancière, the teaching vocation belongs to the realm of emancipation. It consists of revealing to young minds a knowledge that they are called on to interpret. More mysteriously, the teacher's role "is to allow the pupil to reappropriate what he knows without knowing that he has forgotten it."[73]

The work of psychoanalyst Françoise Dolto plays a key role in Winter's thought. Dolto was particularly interested in the appearance of what Lacan calls "the flash"[74] of knowledge in young children—the moment when, after long travails, letters suddenly make words, words make sentences, and sentences make meaning. Logic, born within oneself, quickly leads the child to ask questions that adults rarely bring up: Where do people come from, and why do they die? These fundamental questions accompany the process of learning language; Winter finds many examples of such conjunctions in film or literature.

Beyond these reflections on early childhood, Winter insists on a principle that is valid for all stages of learning: as Lacan says, "too much pedagogical attention"[75] can be detrimental to learning. Winter quotes the example of Marcel Pagnol, who learned to write precociously, and almost passively, simply through proximity to older pupils to whom his father taught the basics of language. These learning practices reveal various mimetic kinds of reading, not confined to the case of young children who pretend to read until meaning appears. The same applies to religious devotees who continuously reread sacred texts that they know by heart and whose scope remains mysterious.

Winter believes that excessively authoritarian teaching becomes an obstacle when it turns a lesson's propositions into "knowledge" that must be strictly reproduced without regard for the process that would enable this reproduction. When they are within the family, he refers to such authoritarian teachers as "educastrators." He also writes: "What matters is not to make things understood, but to see that the obstacles to understanding are removed." Despite appearances, this has little to do with spontaneist and expressionist theories of teaching, which may turn out to be forms of oppression: it is well known that paradoxical commands such as "Be free!" can drive you crazy. This concern leads Winter to provide many examples of wise accompaniment revealing the intelligence of preceptors. In all cases, the teacher is required not to transmit imperatively but to "establish the conditions of transmission," conditions which, to quote Lacan again, help awaken "an insistence in those who are listening."[76]

Ultimately, for Winter, the legacy of teaching has more to do with the responsibility for thinking and questioning than with a strictly positive and utilitarian relation to knowledge. "Above all, transmitting means transmitting a question that remains unanswered."[77]

2

TRADE
AND FINANCE

THE EXHIBITION at the Paris Cité des sciences et de l'industrie was funded by no less an institution than the Banque de France. It was called *L'économie: Krach, Boom, Mue*: this appropriation of jaunty, ironic pop singer Jacques Dutronc's clowning* was intended to bring about a reconciliation between the people and the "economy." An area simulating the stock market had been laid out, and visitors were invited to react "intelligently"—by purchasing or selling shares—to information broadcast by a loudspeaker. The goal was to educate citizens, for, according to economics professor Pierre-Pascal Boulanger (who contributed to the book that accompanied the exhibition), their ignorance of economics is "a threat to democracy."

The exhibition did not merely illustrate what is known as the classical school of "economic science." It gave the impression that behind the experts' vague explanations, there are reasons for recurring crises, junk financial products, the vagaries of the economy, and crazed speculation on

---

* *Krach, Boom, Mue*, which translates as Crash, Boom, Change, is a play on "Crac, boum, hu," a nonsense line from a song by Jacques Dutronc: "Les Playboys."—*CB*.

an overheated stock market. However, these reasons are so complex that ordinary honest citizens cannot really understand them, except through the demeaning channels of popular exhibitions, or perhaps comic strips or TV programs, all filled with pathetic analogies between institutional budgets and the budget of a housewife or paterfamilias. Throughout history, popularization has been a frequent sister of ideology—or counter-ideology, which is not exactly helpful.

But although the market is cluttered with educational material on the economy, other, more caustic discourses are also developing. A small Belgian publishing house, Zones Sensibles, has published two essays by Ervin Karp (a pseudonym), simply entitled *6* and *5*.[1] These essays are not more difficult to read than works presented as accessible, but they provide an original perspective on how the market works now that it has literally lost its head. Similar in intent are a 2013 book on high-frequency trading by Swiss journalists Frédéric Lelièvre and François Pilet,[2] and a 2015 documentary on the "new wolves of Wall Street" directed by Ivan Macaux.[3] All of these works point out that the market now functions without the intervention of the human mind: it is essentially shaped by algorithms whose operations take place within nanoseconds (billionths of a second), and that sometimes go badly wrong. Among other things, algorithms can detect purchase offers on the market and double them, within nanoseconds, in order to take ownership of the shares and sell them at an increased price to whoever originally wanted them. All day long, these electronic stock market wholesalers fling themselves at the speed of light at enormous quantities of securities. The activity generated by such movements puts the whole system at risk. One of the inventors of these machines, Thomas Peterffy, noted in 2010 that they "have evolved more quickly than our capacity to understand or control them."[4] For one thing, unless a natural disaster is involved, it is now impossible to understand "market reactions" to any given piece of political information. "The market" is simply not a social subject anymore. Economic rationality is embodied in computer programs that experts throw into the fray without knowing exactly what will happen to the thousands of billions of dollars that are at stake every day.

On the stock market, these machines play with the savings of people with modest incomes, countries' national debts, and the value of currencies. They have a significant effect on the share prices agencies use to assign crucial ratings to organizations. Karp concludes: "Markets are now nothing but a vast theatre of operations in which human calculators would be unable to understand anything whatsoever."[5] Today, approximately 70 per cent of the stock market transactions carried out in the United States (and 40 per cent of those in Europe) go through these computers, but 90 per cent of purchase offers, which glut the stock exchange and cause prices to go up and down, already belong to them. As an example of what this process can entail, on October 1, 2012, an unidentified algorithm took over the New York Stock Exchange's digital infrastructure by flooding it with pointless offers. The goal was to reduce adversarial flows, as part of a strategy that is still not understood.

Nothing holds together anymore. The New York Stock Exchange is physically located in New Jersey, in the little-known suburb of Mahwah. There, in high-security warehouses the size of several football fields, ultra-high-performing computers fight each other over share values, consuming enough electricity every day to power 4,500 homes. The Paris stock exchange does the same thing; it is located near London, in the little-known town of Basildon.

Any error can have major consequences. On August 1, 2012, an algorithm that the Knight Capital brokerage firm was using for strictly experimental purposes—it was trying to understand how the market would react if an agent suddenly started to behave erratically—went into action on its own in the real New York market. The algorithm bought shares at peak price and sold them when they hit rock bottom. Clients lost $180 per millisecond—that is, $180,000 per second, or $10.8 million per minute—for almost forty-five minutes. Nobody knows why this happened. An equally astonishing event had taken place a few months earlier, on

March 23, 2012, at 14 minutes, 18 seconds, and 436 milliseconds after 11 a.m. A high-frequency trading firm, BATS Global Markets, had just entered the stock market with great fanfare, at an initial share price of $15.25. Within 900 milliseconds, the price had dropped to just $0.28. The firm was knocked out; within a few days, it was forced to accept a takeover by a rival firm. As soon as the share price was announced, an enemy algorithm lying in ambush to destroy the offering had, at break-neck speed, scattered downward purchase offers everywhere. There has been no serious investigation of the terror implied by this financial Wild West of the new century. According to Karp, "This new conflict apparently confirmed that markets are now a battle zone, and that the winner will be the one who owns the fastest and most powerful algorithm."[6]

Recurring crises are the outcome. Experts who still find the business pages meaningful are sleepwalkers. Markets explicitly present themselves as a setting for endless clashes, and traders' bellicose names for their algorithms—Arid, Blast, Guerilla, Iceberg, Nighthawk, Ninja, Shark, Sniffer, Sniper, Stealth, and Sumo—bear witness to the nature of their world. Lobbyists for high-frequency trading explain that this is simply a new kind of Darwinism that will make it possible, eventually, to define market parameters. But the reality is that these algorithms are of no value to us or to our economy as people. What they do is help determine share prices by deceiving each other, covering themselves, carrying out diversionary manoeuvres, or scooping the pot a few microseconds before a rival algorithm can officially capture the prize it had in its sights. The function of Blast, for instance, is to multiply purchase orders on scattered stock exchange platforms in order to block any response from enemy algorithms such as Sniffer, which is programmed to detect operational principles at work in the market. People facing this situation are uneasy. Karp writes that when there is turbulence, traders automatically wonder "if this is an internal bug or if it comes from the market."[7]

This level of agitation produces flash stock market crashes that would leave citizens dumbfounded if their brains could work quickly enough to detect them. Share prices drop to unfathomable depths and are then restored within a microsecond. Markets overheat when a price spirals downwards, then skyrockets back up, and then goes into freefall again. Even when the time span of these dizzying movements can be perceived by human senses, the whole thing seems like a dream. Within ten minutes on May 6, 2010, for instance, US markets lost, then gained, $700 billion. Lelièvre and Pilet, in a chapter entitled "Waiting for the Fatal Crash," describe incredible fluctuations: "Sotheby's share price went from $34 to $10,000, while Accenture Consulting dropped from $40 to one cent."[8] They quote faculty members and financial engineers from France's École Polytechnique who are required to teach these practices to their students, and who are seriously worried by the current frenzy: in their view, the system utterly fails to reach its stated goal, that is, to establish prices. Nicole El Karoui, an eminent mathematician specializing in financial mathematics, describes a system that works in isolation, involving a handful of agents who "don't know where they're going."[9]

This is an economy that we are unable to translate into words. In July 2013, a trader who had abused high-frequency trading software was sentenced to a heavy fine, under the Dodd-Frank banking reform act, by the US Commodity Futures Trading Commission, which is responsible for regulating the derivatives market. The trader had used a trading software program designed to illegally place orders to buy futures and then immediately cancel them. The goal was to artificially draw attention to shares the trader had previously acquired. The penalties imposed in such cases are negligible: today's stock exchange is a genuine war zone in which prices are determined by participants' assets and instruments. They do serve the purpose of mystifying the public, for randomly indicting someone and making an example of him is a way of pretending that exceptions at the periphery are disturbing a system that in itself is working as it should.

Programs intended to educate the public are similarly intended to prevent us from understanding that the system is in complete disarray.

Overall, we might say about the economy what the landlady in Kafka's *The Trial* says of the court system: "It seems like something scholarly, I'm sorry if that sounds stupid, but it seems like something scholarly that I don't understand, but that I don't need to understand either."[10] In fact, we are asked to believe that there is a science of economics at work in the decisions of the powerful people on whom we depend, and that democracy means making citizens into partners who are able to master the vocabulary and basic principles of this "science"—not to act on it in any way, but to be imprisoned in it. This explains the intensive nature of popularization initiatives, whether they are carried out by official institutions and the right-wing press or by grassroots movements or alternative economics publications that provide a critical perspective on the words that are colonizing our world. One problem remains: throughout all of these representations, we are forced to start from a terminology that abuses us, but that only a few economists seem able to avoid. Whether they describe themselves as "unorthodox" or "appalled," they still refer to this terminology in contributions that are certainly beneficial, but that provide no more than a kind of critical dubbing.

The stupid economy

In other words, there is nothing surprising about the fact that we are collectively unable to think about "the economy." Where business is involved, suddenly even a minimal level of analysis appears to be beyond us. Money, once we are dealing with amounts that can noticeably affect a crude indicator such as the gross domestic product—which is associated with another fetish, "job creation"—blocks any attempt at thought. The expression "It's the economy, stupid," originally used to structure the rhetoric of Bill Clinton's presidential campaign in 1992, implies that we cannot imagine average citizens being interested in anything other than what they mean by the economy. If we turn the statement around, however, it means that the economy and its mercenary assumptions are making us stupid, preventing our minds from grappling with issues that elude us. It's the stupid economy, in fact.

Like many other media, in 2012, Montreal daily *Le Devoir* reported on a "historic order" received by the Quebec-based Bombardier group to produce "56 Global twin-engine business jets for an estimated $3.1 billion, with options on 86 additional aircraft from the same family for a total value of over $7.8 billion."[11] Bombardier had signed a contract with VistaJet, a company that rents these jets (seating no more than ten passengers) to billionaires seeking "ultimate comfort" as they travel.

How is it that no one has expressed anger at the underlying reality of which this is a symptom? The VistaJet order is a display of excessive spending on the part of multinational corporations and the class of the super-rich, at a time when year after year, governments have forced citizens to accept their programs of austerity and budgetary "restraint," scolding them, in speech after speech, for their spendthrift habits. This contract reminds us that financial corporations—which governments saved from disaster, beginning in 2008, by handing them thousands of billions of dollars, arguing that their bankruptcy would lead to the collapse of entire civilizations—have gone back to their worst habits now that their cash flow has been restored, paying out billions of dollars in bonuses to executives and board members even during years when they posted a deficit, acting like sorcerers' apprentices in creating ultra-speculative financial objects, and indulging in sumptuary displays of wealth such as the purchase or rental of aircraft like Bombardier's Global. In the context of such decadence, VistaJet's founding CEO, Thomas Flohr, rubs his hands with glee.

> Demand is unprecedented. . . . Our customers need to fly point-to-point across the globe, and in many instances at short notice. Whether it's a direct flight from Los Angeles to Shanghai, from London to Luanda or from Kinshasa to Ulan Bator, we are seamlessly

connecting our customers to every corner of the world in unrivalled levels of style and safety.[12]

A Royal Bank of Canada (RBC) expert told *Le Devoir* that "billionaires and executives of top multinationals" have not been affected by the economic crisis and are still rolling in money—or rather, that they are "showing a fine resilience in dealing with the economic context," since one should never lose an opportunity to praise them for their good fortune even if it occurs within an order that operates structurally in their favour.

The "emerging markets" in which VistaJet plans to operate its new jets are to be found in Russia, China, the Middle East, and Africa: all places where the "emergence" of a propertied class able to pay for such aeronautical whims is necessarily related to political corruption, the plundering of public assets, predatory exploitation of natural resources, and other operations akin to those of organized crime. While a recent article in *Forbes* unsurprisingly revealed that US citizens owned the largest number of private jets (12,717), far ahead of silver and bronze medallists Mexico (950) and Brazil (786), the most phenomenal growth rates in private jet ownership between 2006 and 2016 were displayed by two vulgar plutocracies and a tax haven: Belarus (1,200 per cent), the Isle of Man (667 per cent), and Kazakhstan (600 per cent).[13]

Why is this not obvious to us? In 1789 or in 1848, when gilded carriages paraded through the streets of Paris, the abused people of France did not fail to notice that they were the source of the wealth enjoyed by the aristocratic elite. Why are we now so blind? Because it's good for the economy. "Markets seemed to appreciate the announcement: the share price for the parent company, Bombardier Inc., increased by 8 per cent during the day, closing at $3.37."[14] Such mood swings determine what happens to workers, who are dependent on them. If billionaires, or "high net worth individuals" as they are so charmingly described by Merrill Lynch,[15] were to lose some of their capital and cancel these contracts that are marginally beneficial to the plebs, a specialist warns that such "mammoth contracts" would be worth no more than a stock market rumour. They involve "a greater risk of cancellation if the market falls."[16] Let us hope, therefore, that markets and the governments that support them will continue to drive upward the share prices on which these billionaires depend.

Why are we intellectually so inhibited when we are faced with such shocking situations? Because there is no field in which mediocrity rules with more self-assurance than in what it persists in calling "the economy." The trickle-down theory, a fairy tale for children stating that when the wealthiest people become richer, wealth inevitably flows to the community as a whole, has been challenged from every direction, yet experts and academics still loudly endorse it, making it into an article of faith. If weather forecasters were to predict rain as often as economists announce the imaginary trickling down of wealth throughout the world, we would long ago have stopped listening to them. Our brains are so full of this stupidity that we still view rich people as those who create wealth, a small part of which we might hope to grasp for ourselves, rather than as those who appropriate wealth to our detriment.

Producing luxury jets is a misuse of intelligence for trivial ends. The job of an engineer specializing in the design of a luxury jet's cabin is to fill it with every element of social distinction that will not endanger the life of passengers. This person's expertise serves to put game rooms, whirlpool bathtubs, and dining areas into aircraft for the exclusive use of a tiny number of privileged people.

Strictly speaking, the people who dream of these jets and then actually order them are not motivated by a mania for spending, a taste for luxury, or a blind craving for social distinction. They're not just having fun on board, and the fun that they do have is probably more Pavlovian and less sincere than fun as we know it in the humble abodes of the downtrodden. The structural distortions of our oligarchic regime have made these jets essential to those who aspire to rule the world through powerful boards and institutions. David Rothkopf, a proud observer of the world oligarchy, provides a sociological explanation in his book *Superclass:*[17] in the eyes of the powerful, these jets, which perform at a higher level than regular aircraft, are something specifically required by their way of life, just as North American suburbanites do not believe that they are acquiring a luxury object when they buy a car simply to go to work, even if the car is equipped with the latest electronic gadgets. The caste of the super-rich really believes that it has vanquished space and time: active in all circumstances, it has transcended anything that might resemble a waiting room in either spatial or temporal terms. Rothkopf insists that there is nothing excessive about their use of the jets, since the standard airport context, involving delays, stress, and security risks, could be costly for those who see themselves as the sovereign decision-makers of planetary affairs. Oligarchs must have time and the world at their disposal so that they can rule wherever they go. For them, a private jet as a work tool is simply an investment—a risk-management tool.

Bryan Moss, president of VistaJet's competitor Gulfstream, is perfectly clear on what it's all about: his company serves a social class convinced that nothing must resist their will "to do the things they believe they need to do, to go to the places they need to go, to see the people they need to see, to make those decisions that influence how investments are made at the time and in the place they need to."[18] This of course has a cost: maintenance alone will require between $1.25 million and $1.5 million a year for each jet, assuming some five hundred hours of use. There is no going back; staying competitive is an absolute requirement. And the more members of the oligarchy travel in this way, the less disoriented they feel in any given location, because their point of view on time and the world has been developed outside of time and space. From an indistinct position above the clouds or at the top of the highest tower, they create financial objects that enable them to bet on economic outcomes (driving Greek obligations downwards, turning foodstuffs into futures, making the mortgages of insolvent families into hazardous collateralized debt obligations), so that they can massively increase their wealth when everything falls apart.

Rothkopf insists that Gulfstream workers—the same could be said of people who work for Bombardier—are proud to build aircraft for a social class that they will never even approach. They feel that they are among the few "beneficiaries of globalization,"[19] seeing the capitalists' wealth trickle down onto their garden plots. In other words, everyone chooses to be oblivious, including the ordinary readers of journalistic productions as crude as the ones announcing Bombardier's "historic order": these readers may feel empathy for those who have found a job and satisfaction that they are paying taxes (especially since the company itself may not be paying any). So everyone is following at full steam, and high altitude, the terms and ideology of a ruling caste that no longer sees or feels anything. This is a "superclass," as Rothkopf says, a class that outclasses the class regime itself as it literally hovers above all things. And, from this point of view, it is a class that "economizes" all things—meaning that it both creates their economy, and does without them.* It confines everything within the terms of the market and the speculative economy, in order not to see the unbearable situations that this economy provokes. And so, mediated by the narrow criteria of the sciences of accounting and management, and thanks to its faithfully repeated ideology, the oligarchy elevates abject propositions.

Made in China

Down here, it's in front of us. Everywhere. And it's huge. We ought to be staring at it wide-eyed. But it's the other way around: we are collectively unable to see. Some things have a brutal effect—they register with us and we don't say anything. First, the North American oligarchy induced

---

* In French, the expression *faire l'économie de* can be taken to mean both of these things.—*CB*

China to turn its industrial landscape into a vast free zone* in order to produce the world's consumer goods at a discount; now, the oligarchy wants to create a preferential commercial zone in North America to satisfy the expectations of its Chinese business partners. The social state, pursuing its downward spiral, has taken a new turn toward the bottom.

Min Ying Holdings, a leading Chinese financial corporation involved in banking, electricity, insurance, and real estate, with assets worth a billion dollars, will soon develop an international trade centre in North America to support the massive arrival of Chinese entrepreneurs. The goal is to reduce to a minimum the number of local intermediaries between Asian sweatshops and Western consumers. The bridgehead of this establishment is to be located in Quebec: possible locations in the greater Montreal area include Mirabel, Laval, Longueuil, and Varennes.

In Quebec, Min Ying Holdings is working with a Chinese company deployed in Mirabel, the Mirabel International Trading Centre (MITC). Mirabel is already a free zone created by the Quebec government to foster a "leading-edge economy." The free zone is actually a backward-looking initiative providing tax exemptions to companies, and especially aeronautics companies, that settle in Mirabel. In the Mirabel foreign trade zone, the income tax rate is zero, capital tax has been abolished, no contribution is required to the provincial Health Services Fund, and several other types of tax credits and financial support are provided. The MITC was established in the hope of attracting the Chinese international trade centre directly to Mirabel. Now, according to Radio-Canada, it seems to have finally chosen Varennes, after having looked at Longueuil and a site in Laval that offered a larger number of parking spaces.[20] Whether the corporation chooses a suburb to the north or south of Montreal, it will undoubtedly negotiate conditions at least as favourable as those expected in the free zone.

---

* "Free zone" is a term used throughout this book to describe special areas where companies do not have to comply with labour laws, environmental standards, customs regulations, or other laws.—CB

This project is an economic absurdity even in terms of the liberal free-market ideology. North American industrialists have carried out the politically insane project of destroying the continent's manufacturing infrastructure, chiefly by relocating it to China and leaving its own population only jobs in the service sector; now, the mega-shopping centre will remove this last category of jobs. The Quebec lobbyist who initially defended the project, quoted by the *Journal de Montréal* on November 27, 2013,[21] explains that thanks to this commercial hub, "one thousand Chinese companies will relocate to Quebec, eliminating intermediaries," which of course means Quebec merchants and suppliers. "All manufacturing will be carried out in China," and distribution will be carried out all the way into North America by Chinese nationals. The *Journal de Montréal* adds that this project will have an immediate effect on the prices that local competitors will charge for their goods. Referring to a similar centre in Shanghai—a "consumer's paradise" that is a model for the project—the newspaper reports that "it includes over 62,000 stalls presenting over 400,000 products whose sale prices affect market prices." In other words, not only will local merchants no longer be the sole distributors of products, but those who attempt to defy the competition will have to cope with murderously low prices; for instance, they may have to sell a kitchen tool (made by children in China) for fifty cents rather than a dollar if this is the price established by the new merchants.

The lobbyist who originally defended the project in Quebec City was former member of Parliament Roger Pomerleau, who has now handed over his responsibilities in the matter to former Canadian Liberal minister Martin Cauchon; it seems that former Canadian prime minister Jean Chrétien is also involved. In other words, in this affair, three former elected officials may have sold to private concerns the public information they gained while exercising their political functions.

Thanks to this project, part of Quebec will become a free zone of international calibre that will satisfy all the Chinese suppliers who set up their businesses in it. "Business people from all over Canada and the

United States would travel to Laval [or Varennes], rather than China, to sign their deals," says the *Journal de Montréal*. There is good reason to fear that the presence of Min Ying Holdings will accentuate Quebec's own offshore status. Min Ying is used to the permissiveness of offshore jurisdictions: it is registered in Macao, a tax haven of unusual opacity that is part of China itself. Macao specializes in registering corporations; bank secrecy is inviolable and the tax rate is null. The emigration of millionaire Chinese investors is clearly part of the offshore economy. WealthInsight, an information firm specializing in the identification of the wealthiest actors, estimated in 2013 that wealthy Chinese citizens had placed $658 billion in tax havens. These amounts are continually increasing.

Information on this topic is more than marginally interesting: it gives us an idea of the offshore transformation that Canada is going through. The province of British Columbia is developing as a hub for drug trafficking out of Asia; Alberta, imitated by Saskatchewan, is a petro-state; Ontario is the lair of mining corporations that are active throughout the world. Quebec is a mineral state, entirely dedicated to the interests of its extractive industry and now becoming interested in oil; it is home in Canada to Maples, one of the world's largest law firms specializing in the creation of offshore entities, and now, of course, it is hoping for action with the Chinese import/export sector. As for Nova Scotia, it has developed a hiring program that enables firms in Bermuda to entrust ongoing business to Halifax accountants, the owners of these firms having chosen to locate them in Bermuda to benefit from major tax exemptions.[22]

All of this is the work of former members of Parliament, ministers, or even prime ministers, who are familiar with the decision-makers and the mechanisms of government bodies, and whose goal is to make the state apparatus into a machine that will accumulate capital for industrial and financial oligarchs. None of these achievements has been subject to public debate. Better to let the people tear itself to pieces on the subject of identity markers: this is really the only topic that it can grasp.

Experts to the rescue

As soon as oligarchs fall back into their bad habits (corruption, duplicity, and mediocrity), "experts" on their payroll hurry to rescue them. Take the case of the Quebec government when it was embarrassed by a scandal involving Arthur Porter, a hospital administrator accused of fraud who had found refuge in Panama. Any government knows that on television, it can count on scholars of fortune: in this case, Messaoud Abda, professor of administration at the Université de Sherbrooke, and Michel Nadeau, merchant of "governance."* In a televised interview,[23] the two earnestly followed the script regarding the corrupt hospital director, claiming it had been perfectly natural to see him as a man of the utmost dignity and uprightness. Abda, supposedly a specialist on financial crime, stated that Porter's "achievements" were "extraordinary and exemplary." Absolutely, concurred Nadeau: his record was "impeccable." Was he not an African immigrant who had gone to Cambridge; a friend of former prime minister Stephen Harper, who had named him to the committee supervising Canadian intelligence; and also a friend of Quebec premier Philippe Couillard? And had he not previously been advisor to George W. Bush? Abda then enthusiastically agreed with Nadeau: Porter "hung about" the intelligence services and was just as charming as Bernie Madoff.

---

* Alain Deneault has extensively analyzed the word "governance" and its political implications in a previous work, *Gouvernance: Le management totalitaire* (Montreal: Lux, 2013), the first volume of a two-part work of which *Mediocracy* is the second volume. *Gouvernance* focuses on "governance" as embodying a tendency to replace politics with management; under the rule of "governance," all social reality must be subordinated to the management rules of private enterprise. (The spread of the word "client" as a replacement for such concepts as "patient" or "student" is part of the same tendency.) Widely used and accepted in English, "governance" is a term more likely to be challenged in French, as a consequence of a republican tradition in which the idea of a system of political rule based on negotiations between "stakeholders" is seen as flatly contradicting principles of popular sovereignty and the role of citizens in the body politic.—*CB*

But who, except experts in "governance," could find any of this reassuring? True, the word "governance," missing from the mainstream vocabulary up until a few years ago, is now repeated so often that it almost seems to be acquiring substance. People who are not experts, however, fail to see how proximity to oligarchical circles, intelligence departments, and the highest echelons of US power can be construed as a guarantee of high moral standards or commitment to the public good. However that may be, the Quebec elite was apparently "dazzled" by such unquestionable credentials, and our two experts were lacking in any deeper sociological intuition. There was no discussion of influence peddling, lobbying, or mutual favours between the slippery strategists of so many wheeler-dealer networks. Nor did anyone bring up how tax havens are systematically used to conceal fraud. Why bother with such minor details when you can simply pick yourself up, quickly get over your feigned surprise, and explain in great detail what kinds of fraud the interested party may have committed and the reasons behind the whole affair? As it turns out, the science of governance is actually the art of second-guessing and hindsight.

Upstream, efforts are generally made to conceal the more shocking actions of the regime in order to prevent any challenges that might ensue. When press magnate and major investor Pierre Karl Péladeau decided to go into politics and, outrageously, was on the point of becoming leader of the opposition in Quebec, Michel Nadeau hurried to design a system that would enable Péladeau to keep on using his excessive powers in a seemingly legitimate way. Nadeau's meditation on conflicts of interest served only to lubricate the system to stop it from creaking. "There are not many countries in the world where politicians have been forced to give up their main source of income, even [in the case of] owners of media businesses. . . . We must make sure that business people are still able to go into politics," he told Radio-Canada in March 2014, as if corporate ownership were a way of earning a living like any other. Nadeau thought it would be sufficient if Péladeau put his assets in an independent trust, while entrusting his media businesses to a corporation of which he would own less than 50 per cent of the shares. Such virtual barriers would enable a single person to direct the press, cellphone networks, a sports stadium, and "cultural industries," while also playing a leading public role, and throughout all this the really difficult question is never asked or even hinted at: How can our society accept such a concentration of assets and power not only in the hands of a political figure, but even in the hands of any one citizen? Experts in governance techniques are able to transcend questions on such scandals by making them seem completely natural. "In a democracy, think about the former mayor of New York, [Michael] Bloomberg, who is also the owner of one of world's largest information agencies [Bloomberg LP]. After leaving politics, he is still the owner," explains Nadeau, drawing on his repertoire of inspirational examples.[24]

Baltasar Gracián had already nailed these characters in his seventeenth-century work, *El Criticón*:

> Someone who is seen as a scholar without having studied; is a wise man who never does anything tiring; has an impressive beard without having burned the midnight oil; is full of wind but has never shaken the dust from books; is highly enlightened though he has never stayed up late; is covered with glory without ever having worked through the day or the night. In short, he is the oracle of the vulgar and one whom everyone agrees has great knowledge, although they know nothing about it.[25]

Feminist Andrea Dworkin is more brutal: "While gossip among women is universally ridiculed as low and trivial, gossip among men . . . is called theory, or idea, or fact."[26]

Money sickness

For such people, money creates a screen that hides everything. Money has imposed itself in modern culture as a way to calculate average value, ever since it was made into the preferred sign to mediate between goods. This unit of average measurement of values has imposed itself throughout history as a vector of mediocrity. Georg Simmel indicates that by making it possible to establish prices and cause them to vary, money actually enables us to instantaneously measure the average degree of value of a good in relation to all other objects, on the one hand, and, on the other hand, to the degree of sacrifice that we are willing to accept to abolish the average distance that separates us from it. In other words, the average value of things in relation to each other, and in relation to the average will of subjects to cross the average gap separating them from things, is what a monetary price embodies as the result of a calculation that we do not even have to make. The work Simmel carried out at the turn of the twentieth century has nothing to do with vulgar economics. Simmel was interested first and foremost in the social and cultural role of money in modern times—in its capacity to act like a computer before the computer age, enabling us to compare, measure, and assess the compatibility of all things in relation to each other in terms of their potential value—and he was immediately led to investigate the perversions fostered by money. For money, which bears witness to all of these averages, itself becomes the means that enables us to access all things. If we have enough money, we can surmount what separates us from what we want without having to develop any particular strategy. Money is economical: its ease of use means we can "economize"—do without—strategic deliberation. As the means of access to all things, money becomes a super-means. And as a super-means, it has finally imposed itself in history as a paradoxical supreme goal: above all, we seek ownership of this means of access to all things. As Simmel wrote in 1916:

> It is precisely money which, for the majority of men in our culture, has become the supreme end. It is the possession of money which tends to be the ultimate goal . . . of all the purposive activity of this majority. . . . In the mind of modern man, to be in need means not to be in need of material goods, but only of the money to buy them.[27]

Problems begin when we stop seeing money as a medium of value and start to act as if it contains value or is value itself.

> It is surely obvious that this antedating of the final purpose in its most comprehensive and radical form takes place not in the intermediate instances of life but rather in money. Never has an object that owes its value exclusively to its quality as a means, to its convertibility into more definite values, so thoroughly and unreservedly developed into a psychological value absolute, into a completely engrossing final purpose governing our practical consciousness. This ultimate craving for money must increase to the extent that money takes on the quality of a pure means. . . . Its growing importance depends on its being cleansed of everything that is not merely a means, because its clash with the specific characteristics of objects is thereby eliminated. Money's value as a *means* increases with its *value* as a means right up to the point at which it is valid as an absolute value.[28]

To love money, to be attracted by money, is to be smitten with what gives us access to everything, which means that in reality, no matter how illogical it may seem, we are attracted by nothing—or by nothing except the means of obtaining all values, which money reduces to their simplest expression. These values, paradoxically, are forgotten by practical consciousness because money becomes an absolute value. To become attached to this means among all means is to take the medium of value for value itself, and little by little to become attached to a statistic of value that is impersonal, insignificant, undetermined, neutral, and average. We mistake an identikit portrait of value for the thing itself, and prefer the map to the territory. From the point of view of consciousness, money brings everything down to the level of this neutral reference point. This means (*moyen*) of acquiring everything allows us to acquire everything that it makes average (*moyen*).

Unlike Marx, Simmel turned his attention to the psychological consequences of a culture dominated by money as a symbolic fetish. Like capital, but now on a psychological level, money has a distorting effect, because it concentrates the mind's activity on a means that makes it lose all sense-awareness of the world's diversity. In chapter three of *The Philosophy of Money*, Simmel, somewhat in the manner of La Bruyère, offers a portrait gallery of typical figures, including the miser, the spendthrift, the greedy person, the blasé person, and the cynic. Money is at the centre of these personality developments, which it in fact generates. For each of these types, money is an artificial device that enables the mind to cut itself off from empirical reality in favour of disembodied accounting systems. Confirmed at the psychological level, this metaphor has not materialized on the stock exchange as money is disseminated through the limitless reach of a global information network, providing an account of reality ever more distant from the sense-awareness of a narrative, even though the word "account" can mean both "story" and "record of credit and debit entries." Onscreen data now have force of law. Only sterile balance sheets, presented as immaculate tables or unanswerable bookkeeping columns, now justify an economy that we are no longer able to see in any other way. We become sick from being held at a distance from economic operations that could once be grasped by the senses, at a time when these operations involved strategies to reduce the gap that separated us as subjects from the objects of our desire. Now that acquisition strategies have been transposed to the monetary level, we economize (do without) the world. This harms us, and the generalized repression we are experiencing does not leave our world unharmed, either.

First, avarice. The person affected by this trait contemplates the virtual fortune promised by the monetary sign, holding back from letting it materialize as anything. Better to fantasize about the countless acquisitions money promises than to convert it into a single one of them. The miser demands that monetary signs provide him with all of the enjoyment it announces without necessarily engaging in an actual experience in which enjoyment would be put to the test. The miser wants to experience "the abstract form of enjoyment which, none the less, is not enjoyed,"[29] he asks money to enjoy in his place. Because he has the power to do "everything," he is released from the obligation of actually being able to do anything, and is protected from any disappointment associated with a test. Money legitimates fantasies of limitless possibilities, providing the illusion that everything can be effortlessly given concrete form. This attitude is based on the powers that money embodies in modern culture. It is at the same time "noticeable"[30] and absolutely unfamiliar; culturally it is seen as the absolute and abstract sign of value, and as such it strikes our imagination as "pure energy."[31]

The spendthrift, on the contrary, cares nothing for such symbols: he wants to taste the fruit of the promise, no matter what the cost. Could it be said that the miser and the spendthrift live under the same regime, the one doing the opposite of the other? Without denying the affinities between the two, we note a qualitative difference that makes this comparison, strictly speaking, difficult. The miser clutches at monetary signs, consolidates them, and requires their merciless accuracy, to the point where he is overcome by delusions of grandeur in which money is seen as the only criterion for access to power, as in Balzac's *Eugénie Grandet*. The spendthrift attitude, on the other hand, consists of sovereign denial of all institutions that work to ensure the recognition of monetary value. No privative term is sufficient for Simmel as he attempts to describe the spendthrift's carefree attitude and social nonchalance, noting his complete loss of signposts regarding relatedness, measure, or limits (*Beziehungslosigkeit, Maßlosigkeit, Grenzenlosigkeit*), and the demands that he sees no reason to restrict, since he himself remains utterly deformed. All of this is deployed with unbridled violence. The figure of Shakespeare's Timon of Athens comes to mind.

The greedy person now steps forward. He does not seem to embody a type; rather, he is characterized by the moral disorder and state of confusion in which he plunges as soon as money is available to him. Greed necessarily occurs in contexts where money can no longer be associated with any kind of merit, where we do not know what "money" means when it is released from its hinges and represents only the sum of the fantasies that it crystallizes. This is the case, for instance, when money is inherited, when someone makes a killing on the stock market, or when a corporate executive is given a fantastically large bonus. This money is not associated with any work, any achievement of any kind, any formal process. At this point, violence is unleashed. The money seems directly connected to the unconscious, and it gives rise to the lowest passions: jealousy, hatred, aggression, resentment, fear, covetousness.

The sickness of the blasé person is caused by income security. Having received the wages that he earned through repetitive and standardized actions, he languishes as a consumer in a system where everything is also acquired through recurring gestures: putting coins on a counter or signing a cheque. His way of gaining access to goods puts him at a considerable distance from the vitalist principle. "The blasé person . . . has completely lost the feeling for value differences. He experiences all things as being of an equally dull and grey hue."[32] Since the value of a thing is notably determined by the real efforts that you must make to obtain it (a glass of milk does not have the same value if you pay for it at the café or if you must find a cow), as long as you have the monetary means of obtaining an object of desire without any particular effort (by putting a bill or a few coins down on a counter), the thing you acquire is depreciated in psychological terms. Value appreciates according to distance and to what must be done to surmount this distance. "The object thus formed, which is characterized by its separation from the subject, who at the same time establishes it and seeks to overcome it by his desire, is for us a value," says Simmel in *The Philosophy of the Money*.[33] The less you have to find ingenious ways of accessing goods—since money is sufficient for each operation—the more the process employed to reach your ends becomes indifferent. The "charms" of the goods are all the more likely to "fade away"[34] in that the path leading to consumer goods does not provide any kind of excitement.

The cynic also presents himself as a depressive figure. Unlike the spendthrift, he appreciates the things of the world in an absolutely equal manner, as if their possible translation into money neutralized their specific qualities.

> His awareness of life is adequately expressed only when he has theoretically and practically exemplified the baseness of the highest values in the illusion of any differences in values. This mood can be most effectively supported by money's capacity to reduce the highest as well as the lowest values equally to one value form and thereby to place them on the same level, regardless of their diverse kinds and amounts.[35]

Reducing everything to a monetary quantity is associated with an inability to consider value except according to such accounting standards. The cynic judges every form of value exclusively in the light of the monetary sign, without any political, ethical, or, as we notice today, environmental consideration.

The contrast between all and nothing, fostered by money, produces a mindset that tends to disinvest the objects of the world. Simmel found only one cause for rejoicing during World War I: bread coupons distributed in lieu of money enabled the community to return to an awareness of the noticeable value of things rather than the value of their equivalents.

We leave the appreciation of things behind when we force ourselves to go through money to measure value. The culture of money conceals reality behind a screen. The capitalist culture in which value is a matter of financial assets and luxury objects for rich people, and for poor people and average consumers a matter of bargains and quality/price comparisons, has led to the development of specific pathologies. It has made some people structurally miserly and cynical, others blasé and greedy. Major investors and oligarchs display all the characteristics of Grandet, who, in his study, contemplates his mountain of gold while members of his household are sick and hungry. We see them in highly indebted countries, and among impoverished populations, plotting twisted new moves to increase the value of their share portfolio, their real estate assets, and other obscure documents that are preserved offshore. Indifferent to the misery of the world, which has been dropped into the forgotten abyss of "externalities" by the accounting categories to which their conscience is restricted, everything for them is a matter of arithmetic, as if numbers, far from translating cries and suffering, now had a value in themselves and belonged exclusively to a game. The middle class is caught up in the game, unable to develop a different perspective on an order from which it obtains only random benefits, without mastering the rules: it stays at home, a home that seems to offer it asylum and where it hopes that it will continue to enjoy—for a time—the goods whose mode of expropriation it never completely controls. The stereotypical behaviour of this class becomes a way of confirming its submission: it adopts an average behaviour in order to obtain small means, and is continually threatened with becoming blasé. Escape into entertainment or easily prescribed psychoactive substances reveal the ills with which it is permanently threatened.

Poor people, and the peoples of Africa or elsewhere that capital mercilessly colonizes, are also threatened by greed, given the ways they are subjugated by the Western culture of money. In such places, money seems to come from nowhere and always to be destined for distant countries. It is passing through. Money is known to be invested with value, but only in terms of forms, considerations, and realities foreign to the economic life with which it is associated. Because funds are not produced by the organization of the community itself, money seems predestined to be embezzled or used as a bribe. Because the Western cultural order has imposed its game of money on the world, and thus corrupted it, things present themselves everywhere in this way.

The greedy economy

When you hold a coin between your thumb and forefinger, what are the connections that give it meaning? The coin is associated with the value of the goods and services that it enables you to relate to each other: a loaf of bread, a bus ticket, an electric kettle, an apartment rental, a sweater, candles, and so on. But a stable authority is required to establish the value of the coin itself within a certain radius: this is what enables it to keep changing shapes as it helps you assess one commodity and then another. In other words, the coin is connected not only with a set of values associated with commodities, but also with a point of gravity that guarantees its orbit— the orbit that will create a circular order for the activity of the community that uses it. This conceptual whole is known as the "economy."

What happens when the centre of gravity is cruelly lacking? If money goes through a community with the speed of an arrow, coming in from one side and going straight out the other, without creating concerted motivations or a concentrated economy, then what? This is what we see in a number of African countries, for instance. Squandering and corruption are the outcome. The currency that has since 1945 been legal tender in former French colonies in western and central Africa is itself a sign of the economic decentring that is the source of all dysfunction. Fifteen countries use the CFA franc. CFA, which stands for African Financial Community, until recently meant French Colonies in Africa, and this currency enabled France to manage its business in conquered territories in a uniform manner. Its value for many decades was defined in relation to the French franc, until the latter was absorbed by the euro. Even today, Africa's two "franc zones" ensure the legal value of a currency that is really a "countervalue," with a fixed parity link to the euro. It is guaranteed not by any African central bank but by the French Treasury, according to a European Union decision enshrined in the 1992 Maastricht Treaty. In *L'Afrique au secours de l'Afrique*,[36] Senegalese economist Sanou Mbaye does not hesitate to describe the CFA franc as a "colonial relic," noting that only dictators find this currency advantageous, since its convertibility into French francs or now into euros supports capital flight.

Beyond the issue of who controls the currency is the issue of who controls investment. Capital whose value is assessed elsewhere is also, logically, invested from abroad. Although Africa is rich in resources, as long as it lacks infrastructure and allows foreign organizations to plunder its goods, it cannot shape a strong economy for itself. As a consequence, money circulating in the region often does not draw value from the realities of production and exchange that belong to the community involved.

Financial capital, on the contrary, appears in a magical form, not associated in any way with the state of work, production, or distribution of goods in an organized society, but rather with Africans' ability to attract and, more importantly, to appropriate them. Overall, the funds come from three sources. First, the budgets of international funders intended for "development"—a word too often used ideologically to imply that Africa needs to catch up with the West. Then, private investments—on the part of agri-food, mining, oil, pharmaceutical, and other companies—that rain down in passing on high-ranking state officials and, erratically, on a few of their subordinates; the latter support entire clans consisting of family, friends, and contacts. Lastly, the social economy, periodically providing the arbitrary plenty of assistance programs and so-called non-governmental organizations. To channel funds to themselves, people in Africa will sometimes, even if they are not convinced, take up the language of white Samaritans in order to win their favour. Representatives of African NGOs will learn to speak social-democratish or sing communist, enliven their demands with anti-globalization mantras, or formulate requests using the empty words of governance, depending on whether they are attempting to charm a foundation affiliated with a European socialist party, a radical far-left foundation, a conventionally minded NGO, or a department of the World Bank.[37]

The problem is not the family or clan structure, but its hybrid association with technicist Western capitalism. No longer a form of organization like any other, the clan structure has now become an instrument of parasitical appropriation, the only way to extort from imperialist forces some part of the wealth that these forces are plundering.

Economic colonization of this kind leads to discouragement, and in some cases this may be a deliberately pursued outcome. An extraordinary documentary by Paul Cowan and Amer Shomali, *The Wanted 18*,[38] relates such a story taking place in the Middle East: the Israeli state imposes a curfew on a Palestinian community, seeking to seize eighteen dairy cows that provide the villagers with a fragile degree of economic self-sufficiency. A brutal picture emerges of an imperial economic order that knowingly distinguishes between two camps, those who make money and those who ask for it. At each extremity of the spectrum, we find on the one hand the very wealthy, multinationals, expatriates, and local potentates, who abuse their privileges, and on the other, poor people who have often lost any strategic way out of their condition. At the centre is the junction between those who are parasites on institutions (customs, media, civil service, security), taking whatever they can here and there through stratagems of low-level daily corruption, and those who attempt to establish a modest degree of financial self-sufficiency and who may find that people around them appropriate the modest profits they are able to make. "I'm supposed to support the development of an independent agricultural co-operative," explains a Western intern in Togo. The project seems relevant in that it does not require any technical infrastructure that is inaccessible to local farmers. "We supply land, tools, and startup capital. But it's not working. Most of the people we deal with are basically asking us for money." Why? Self-sufficiency, when achieved on a very small scale, leads to a whole set of peripheral problems that can end up being even worse than precarious dependency. If a people is to be released from the culture of handouts in which it is plunged by economic colonialism, this will not be done bit by bit, by targeting one small group of women or farmers, or one auto repair co-operative, but by including society as a whole.

What is true of the currency is also true of political and cultural references. In Africa, so-called French-style republics are actually an insult to political life: their geopolitical frontiers are a direct legacy of the colonial period. Western Africa is still largely dominated by an imperialist matrix, even if Western African states are officially independent. Interference has already taken place even before troops are sent in, rebel groups are instrumentalized, elections are rigged by secret services, diplomats peddle influence, or multinationals step in to bribe ministers and civil servants. In Western Africa, it is structural. Colonial powers haunt the territory thanks to the enduring shape they have given to the area's political regimes.

Many of these regimes present themselves as caricatures of the French Fifth Republic, which was itself, in 1958, the apotheosis of De Gaulle's monarchical fantasies. The concentration of power in the hands of a single person (which is finally being denounced today in France) has reached all-time highs in former French colonies in Africa under dictatorships that are disguised as democracies with the blessing or even the active support of France and other Western powers. These regimes display, in intensified form, all of the flaws of the Fifth Republic. Not only are heads of state empowered to appoint the country's prime minister and ministers, and to dissolve legislatures at will; they can also—and this is a constitutional aberration—take over ministers' responsibilities, including strategic portfolios such as Defence or the Interior. Who are the "citizens" who might recognize their will in such a power structure? It bears an uncanny resemblance to the one that emancipation movements specifically set out to destroy when they achieved independence. The fact that these regimes, with their outdated geographical boundaries, are generally organized as clans, lineages, ethnic groups, or local families, with the Gnassingbés or the Bongos as prime examples, does not in any way imply that the population feels it is well represented. The idea of the common good is nothing but a rhetorical fiction.

Such national structures are manipulated from the outside. Orders, institutional models, financial flows, and great figures all arrive from abroad, in relation to goals that are also determined by what happens abroad. Consequences are well known and are confirmed, year after year, by Global Financial Integrity: every year, tens of billions of dollars leave the continent through illegal or criminal channels ($50 billion per year according to the last evaluation, and $1,000 billion over the past fifty years).[39] These amounts are much larger than the development "aid" funds that rich countries grant so generously. Over time, one strategy becomes central for African populations: take what you can from passing financial flows, channel the benefits of institutions that make up the state apparatus toward your own network, use charm to obtain windfalls from NGOs and cunning to get residual local funding from internationally supported programs. Clans are highly experienced players: they have had a long time to develop responses to foreign modes of intervention. Although this kind of reflex will ultimately lead a society to disaster, the fact that they appropriate foreign funds cannot simply be attributed to corruption: it is actually a form of resistance. There is no need to add to opprobrium by denouncing each stratagem intended to channel into local networks the money that foreign investors and funders chiefly intend to serve the purposes of colonial exploitation. The West has placed these Africans in a humiliating position: they are like participants in a degrading TV show that puts people in a glass box and requires them to lunge at paper money blown about by a fan.

Remote-controlled looting

Populations in the global South no longer know to whom they can turn; they don't know if there is even something called "government" making decisions anymore. In Haiti, "non"-governmental organizations have the shady look of a political occupation force. They are everywhere and decide everything, their forces knowingly scattered. "Governance" asserts itself once again: we can't figure out where power is located. Since the 2010 earthquake, a microcosm of humanitarianism has been living—and sometimes living very well—off the Haitian catastrophe. It is often funded by the private foundations created by businesses that are either rebuilding the country, fragment by fragment, or planning how to plun-. der its natural resources. The result is a topsy-turvy situation in which humanitarian action, although it is strictly palliative, marginalizes the government to the point where the people no longer remember even the idea of a public institution. How, in any case, could they believe in such a thing when political power throughout Haitian history has presented itself only in the form of violent kleptocracies or foreign powers? The era of Haiti Open for Business has unambiguously begun. In this context, humanitarian aid is a minimal investment through which foreign inves- tors hope that one of the world's poorest populations will be brought to support a model of economic activity that continues to harm it.

Immediately after the January 2010 earthquake, the Interim Haiti Reconstruction Commission (IHRC) put the country under de facto trusteeship, restricting the government to a strictly formal role. Former American president Bill Clinton co-chaired this motley entity consisting of private companies, NGOs, funding agencies, countries with a history of political interference in Haiti, and a few representatives of local authori- ties and labour unions. The Haitian prime minister's role as co-chair was intended to improve IHRC's image. Economist Fritz Deshommes describes the commission as a sovereign body, "strange and bizarre, that can sign contracts with anyone it likes; grant or withhold land, operating licences, or investment authorizations; approve or reject projects, with- out being accountable to anyone."[40]

In a country that has been through many trials, no authority at that time was able to look at common issues from a general point of view. Improvements could only be piecemeal: foundations provided money to build a clinic here, pave thirty feet of road there, build a haphazard library somewhere else. All of these achievements were duly credited to the companies or NGOs that provided the services, as garish billboards proclaimed. Overall, the literacy rate remained unchanged, city street networks were still devastated, and sanitation problems were as serious as ever; and the state and any other institution designed for the common good now seemed to have more or less vanished. Not that this matters: in a governance regime, the only things that count are partnerships between the various and unequal members of "civil society" (a sanitized term that must always be given preference over expressions such as "citizens" or "the people"), the private sector, and a state now viewed as no more than a peer. Disorder thus becomes the locus of authority. One organization renovates a cultural centre that has no staff and no books, another sends a dysfunctional ambulance to Port-au-Prince, and a third provides beds for a hospital that is unable to receive them. Funders create projects to take young children off the street, but the children go back to the street when they turn twelve, since no other program is designed to provide continuity with the first one. According to communication professor Luné Roc Pierre Louis, everything is done "case by case," with no value system to structure social activity.

However, since survivors still smile on glossy NGO brochures, the managers of wretchedness still peacefully balance the accounts on which their conceit is based. The US dollar transcends the babble of languages spoken by development workers who have withdrawn to the suburb of Pétionville. They see Port-au-Prince through the prism of their limited knowledge and the tinted windows of their handsome cars. Their logos dominate neighbourhoods like opaque signatures. Scribblers and barkers provide justification by peddling, once again, the idea that the Haitian people are cursed: apparently an unknown divinity has decided that Haiti will always be a basket case. Such thoughts bring peaceful dreams to the Samaritans of capital.

Haiti for them is a humanitarian bubble worth ten billion dollars. What will they do with this amount of money? In a country accustomed to laxity, corruption, and abuse of power, the question does not even arise: with some exceptions, these are people who drop in, make sure they are paid, and leave. This new type of colonial domination is documented by Justin Podur in his book *Haiti's New Dictatorship*,[41] and by Nikolas Barry-Shaw and Dru Oja Jay in *Paved with Good Intentions*.[42]

Raoul Peck also explains in his documentary *Fatal Assistance*[43] that it was difficult to find sponsors to pay for cleaning up the debris from the 2010 earthquake, because this part of the work was not "seductive" from an advertising point of view. It is far more profitable, and the photos are better, if you put up a ramshackle school building and fill it with happy children.

After the positive side, Haitians discovered the pragmatic side of governance: the mining projects that NGO billboards tried to conceal. The rhetorical, technical, and financial culture of the West operates by establishing a distance that leads to irresponsibility. The time is past when gold seekers, foolhardy, feverish, and delirious, stepped over their comrades' dead bodies to set up their wretched camps in the Klondike's hostile winter. Back then, they hoped to extract from the soil a few nuggets that would change their lives—which were not worth much more. Today's gold adventurers are faraway investors. Hidden behind computer screens in their quiet offices, they expose others to the worst perils, endangering lives and ecosystems that are not theirs. They no longer set out to do battle themselves: battles are waged by their lobbyists, lawyers, engineers, accountants, communications experts, local intermediaries, and militias. The dynamite, the drills, the trucks, the creators, the cyanide, and the slag heaps are theirs. Their motorized omnipotence is heard in the roaring of a terrifying rumour: a gigantic economic Frankenstein is about to pump water at a location where water is already worth gold. The word DEVELOPMENT will be printed above stereotypical faces on the NGO billboards surrounding the site— NGOs funded by company foundations. Later, people will remember the sardonic smirk of the dream sellers while breathing in clouds of toxic particles and dust and coughing up their lungs. Development propaganda will replace the old landscape and its lost vitality.

In Haiti, the wheeler-dealers transmute contempt into smiles as they speak of "co-operation," "solidarity," and "friendship." Notice how affected the ambassador looks when he shakes people's hands. Notice how intimidating the mining lobby appears when it explains the pitiless terms of its mechanical science to members of the Haitian National

Parliament. Take a look at the glossy corporate publications in which Majescor glowingly describes its prospects, and notice how it feels when palliative aid projects start to close in on you.

It's a far step to *Masters of the Dew*, the 1944 novel by Haitian writer Jacques Roumain[44] in which the hero struggles against "superstition" to encourage his people to share and develop sources of water. Today, we have entrepreneurs of the dew, the Canadian investors who have burst onto the scene, always in touch with their own frenzied loa, the vodun spirits of finance. Nothing can distract them: the spirit of infinitely multiplied gain has made them lose their heads. They'll destroy everything for the sake of gold that will end up in the vaults of central banks—gold, the ultimate fetish guaranteeing the value of the market securities and scriptural money in which they themselves hardly believe. Any increase in their own share prices will lead their shareholders to encourage the worst possible behaviour, which makes the whole thing even more absurd.

Gold mining requires staggering quantities of water: thousands of litres per minute. This is especially the case in high-tonnage, low-grade mines involving enormous amounts of waste for every few grams of ore extracted. Canadian mining company Albert Mining Inc. is not trying to hide anything: the entrepreneurs of the dew will recklessly exploit water resources. Albert (formerly known as Majescor), a member of the SOMINE consortium, lays claim to a 50 km² site located thirty kilometres southeast of Cap-Haïtien.[45] An official report carried out for the company notes that the Fraîche River is the only year-long source of water on the property, and that wells will be required to ensure a constant supply of water at all times. The river, which flows to Trou-du-Nord, may already be threatened. According to a study carried out by American hydrologists, some of the area's streams and rivers are already contaminated by industrial sites.

For the corporation, twenty billion dollars in profits is at stake. For the Haitian population, the mining project is more likely to entail wholesale destruction. If the usual script plays out, the opening of the mine will lead to demographic destabilization: people from neighbouring communities who hope to get a job will stop working the land, leading to local tensions. Clinics will no longer be sufficient to deal with emergencies, prostitution will be the only new growth sector (there will also be rapes), and public health problems will arise. It will eventually become clear that good jobs are for expatriates and that the local people are to be assigned low-level, low-wage work. Bribes paid out to local potentates will prove to be significantly greater than any royalties or taxes that might benefit the population as a whole.

In economic terms, attention is rarely paid to the price that the state must pay to develop a territory to accommodate the demands of the extractive sector. Maintaining the road network, ensuring the availability of water and electricity, managing the judicial system, maintaining a police force and public administration to guarantee access to property: all of these require funds that as a consequence are not available to develop institutions in the public interest. The technical achievements associated with the open-air mining project in the Cap-Haïtien region could be carried out in such a way as to provide access to water for the entire population. But the voices of finance dictate other priorities.

A neighbouring mining site in the Dominican Republic, in the eastern part of the island of Hispaniola, is worth considering. The Pueblo Viejo site is the extension of the mineral deposit that Albert hopes to exploit in Haiti. Two Canadian companies, Barrick Gold and Goldcorp, are working the site. Since extraction began in 2012, the population has accused them of polluting 2,500 m³ of water per hour, in a region where access to drinkable water is very limited for 20 per cent of the population. Extraction implies that 24,000 tons of material is treated with cyanide every day. The population is afraid that the companies will dump cyanide waste in the Dominican Republic's largest water reserve, which would hardly be without precedent in the somber annals of the mining industry. The Dominican police force protects Barrick's mine and has not hesitated to use violence against demonstrators, who do not know how to end the process.

The public purse will profit only marginally from this forty-billion-dollar project. The government's 17.5 per cent royalty rate may seem significant, but most of the royalties will not be paid until shareholders have received their due, and this percentage is dependent on the price of gold not dropping below $1,400 per ounce. Also, Barrick has undertaken to launch a program to clean up a river contaminated by Placer Dome, a company Barrick acquired in the Dominican Republic, and the cost of this program will be deducted from the royalties. "Barrick will recover 100 per cent of its investment," explains *La Presse* journalist Hugo Fontaine, who adds that the corporation is also "exempt from a wide range of taxes, including municipal taxes."[46] What will remain of these announcements, except their harmful effects?

The gold industry's smooth talkers are promising, of course, that the operations of the Haitian mine will be clean. When have imperial powers ever openly boasted that they are going to pulverize the ecosystems of an abused population? Albert, a company mainly involved in exploration work, is the pilot fish that will carry out preliminary work around the deposit so that a multinational can later ensure its technical exploitation. "Once Majescor [Albert] has finished its surveys, the company will look for a major partner, like Barrick Gold or Newmont, to carry out the extractive part of the project," writes Fontaine.[47] Based on the way it played out in the Dominican Republic, things aren't looking too good for Haiti.

Another element is that the Haitian mining project is close to the Caracol free zone, whose development has already brought misfortune to the area, depriving peasants of the best arable land. Hundreds of expropriated families have paid the price for this operation. Free zone workers also pay a price: in 2013, local journalist Jean Jores Pierre wrote that "at the end of the working day, some workers do not have more than 57 gourdes (US$1.36) of the 200-gourde (US$4.75) daily wage."[48] Some compare the textile factories in the free zone to Asian sweatshops.

In the realm of finance, great minds are destined to meet. The conjunction of the two projects, free zone and mine, will probably justify the creation of a deepwater port that would endanger a marine ecosystem. Can you develop a region while you are destroying it? The answer would seem to be yes, as long as nothing is destroyed on the imaginary plane. People speak of a "Haitian Eldorado" so that we will keep on dreaming, not thinking. Marketing obliterates the counterproductive nature of the destruction and turns our attention away from the industry's ill-advised use of water. The millions of dollars that the mining group is thinking of investing create such mystification that the region's agricultural potential is completely forgotten. Images, images, images. When people are hungry, how can they resist the mirage of "job creation"—even when it is the prelude to territorial destruction, and mostly benefits Western expatriates who will live in isolation in their expensive hotels?

If today's masters of the dew can resist intimidation, the temptation of apathy, and the call of corruption, they will be able to take a stand on a principle that goes beyond the arguments of seasoned lobbyists: the precautionary principle. Elected officials cannot be justified in exposing their people to such risks, especially when the benefits are so paltry for Haitian citizens. There can be no justification for shaping the institutions of the common good solely in terms of private interests.

In this regard, the following resolution of the Haitian Senate, dated February 20, 2013, is exemplary.

> Given the genocide that accompanied the plundering of our mineral resources in the 15th century;
>
> Given the organized sale of our national heritage during the period of the American occupation;
>
> Given the country's current inability to carry out confident negotiations regarding its mineral resources during a time of political imbalance, and while the government is further weakened by the military occupation of the national territory by multinational forces;
>
> Given the waste of resources already recorded in non-priority areas following the earthquake of January 12, 2010, caused by the lack

of a national consensus regarding the challenge of reconstruction;
Given the opacity surrounding the gross value of the ore, and evaluations and estimates regarding already identified resources;
. . .
Considering the serious environmental risks attached to this kind of activity, and given the already alarming level of degradation of our environment.
. . . Therefore, the Senate of the Republic adopts the present resolution and expressly and solemnly asks the Executive to:
Article 1: immediately stay the execution of exploitation permits already issued to SOMINE S.A. . . .[49]

Unfortunately, this text is not law and the unspoken motivations of those who had the merit of voting for it have not all been made clear. However, it does reveal the strength of character that can be shown by a people through the institutions responsible for mediating the people's will. Rather than setting everything up so that the territory can be drained by upholders of financial abstractions, the goal is to ward off the angels of death to whom these apostles of perversity pay allegiance. For Haitians still experiencing the pulse of human rhythms, and who have a deep sense of belonging to their difficult land and its all too rare offerings, the arrival of these frenetic new believers calls urgently for resistance.

Labour unions "fighting" their comrades throughout the world

Faced with worldwide exploitation, labour unions have not proved capable of consolidating workers' fronts on a sufficient scale. In discourse as in thought, every alternative is blurry. Investors and industrialists are even able to present themselves as the victims of international competition, extending a hand to the labour movement so that workers will have compassion on them and agree to share their fate. The basis for this is often the competition required by our ultraliberal model—a model that labour unions should never, under any circumstance, support. "Competition forces us to take measures all very unpleasant. But we are under pressure from globalization. We have to compete with people who get very small wages," states a powerful Austrian investor, Mirko Kovats, in Erwin Wagenhofer's documentary *Let's Make Money*.[50] "It is quite simple, we have to work more. We have no choice," says Kovats, putting himself in the same category as workers whose mandatory overtime hours are not paid, as if he and they belonged to the same social group and were joined in the same adventure. This employer, like the oligarchy as a whole, has enthusiastically shaped the wretched working conditions of the subordinates with whom he rhetorically associates himself. The documentary shows him lauding his facilities in India—another country that is Open for Business—because a worker's wages, at a cost "that is far below Europe," require a modest investment of 250 euros per month, or at most, 2,500 euros for highly qualified personnel such as engineers. And yet this is still too much, according to our asset-holding friend. "We can't afford to be generous," he smugly intones, contemplating the technical structure of his factory—which makes it possible to minimize human participation in the work—as one might review, at the university, a case study illustrating the Marxist critique of political economy.

Two books, Ghislaine Raymond's *Le partenariat social*[51] and Jean-Marie Pernot's *Syndicats: Lendemains de crise?*,[52] explain how Western labour unions have come to believe in the identification between the interests of workers and those of employers that Kovats tries to embody with his specious "we"—an identification that was a leitmotif of 1990s ideological discourse. Raymond's book shows how the 1996 socio-economic summit organized in Quebec City by Lucien Bouchard's Parti Québécois government, at the labour movement's request, trapped unions in a logic of "partnership" with government and big business. "Globalization" has profoundly modified the bonds of solidarity established by the labour movement: suddenly, companies that exploit union members have become their allies, while international comrades—who, were the companies to relocate, might be hired by the same companies—are seen as rivals. Determined to take a position at the global level, the labour movement has abandoned the combative unionism that once ensured its solidarity with the international working class: in Quebec as in many other places, it now stands with employers against their foreign rivals. At the socio-economic summit, labour leaders did not bat an eye when they were given only 8 per cent of the speaking time, with the lion's share going to the premier and the business leaders who made up the great majority of attendees. Labour union investments as shareholders in Quebec companies—a prime example is the Fonds de solidarité of the FTQ, Quebec's largest labour union—help befuddle people's thinking and make their strategies incoherent.

The failures that labour organizations experienced at the summit are exhaustively documented by Ghislaine Raymond. While demanding that the Quebec government stimulate the economy by aiming for full employment and raising taxes on big business, the unions agreed to a diametrically opposed position. In the end, the government froze the minimum wage, abolished some forty thousand jobs in the civil service and the healthcare system, slashed public services, and raised fees for services rather than the corporate tax rate. Raymond finally notes that, with the labour unions' approval, it was stated that "the government will be able to modify the collective agreements of government employees to adjust them to cuts being carried out in public services, without this being seen as a reopening of collective agreements."[53] The unions gained only one thing, a pay equity law designed to equalize the pay for jobs predominantly occupied by women and by men: this, of course, is at most a remedy for a historic injustice. In France, and elsewhere, labour unions have been forced to realize that the "rules of social partnership" under neoliberalism structurally reduce them to mere lobbies. The "social dialogue" to which they are invited along with other members of "civil society" (who else?) seems designed to have them endorse decisions that have already been made. The social conference organized by the socialist government of France in 2014 was a farce, as noted in an interview by French political scientist Jean-Marie Pernot:

> These conferences were supposedly intended to produce viable social compromises that could be adapted to different businesses and departments. We are very far from this, despite the abundance of collective bargaining that takes place within our social relations. We are giving a performance: it's really about the government providing a roadmap for "social partners" so that it can farm out the job of carrying out its policies. Usually, they are given three months to redesign the labour market or pension plans; the government lets them know what it expects, and will take the matter back in hand if it doesn't get it.[54]

This kind of structural defeat is far more serious than any failed strike, since it breaks the labour movement's core subjectivity. The movement has lost its voice without getting anything back for it, except to become a minor partner in an ultraliberal financial system that only benefits the most powerful. In some places, union members will now be able to benefit from union investments as shareholders, while contemplating their leaders' political impotence.

The labour movement seems to have lost sight of any independent strategic orientation; instead, it has focused on accompanying bewildered individual workers in their disarray. Labour activists today must compete with contradictory forms of subjectivity promoted by the dominant ideology: the subjectivities of avid consumers, people with an accounting mindset, misers entirely focused on their own interests, narcissists with an atomized psyche and no expectation beyond the horizon of their summer cottage. Powerful advertising resources have been used to caricature union members, and nothing has been done to provide a contrasting sociological description that would reflect their real conditions. So the general impression prevails that they are identical to a middle class that is consistently presented as mediocre. This image all too often coincides with C. Wright Mill's deadly description in *White Collar:* the group described by Mills is unable to unite around a view of the world that would make them into active subjects. According to Mills, the white-collar man is "pushed by forces beyond his control, pulled into movements he does not understand; he gets into situations in which his is the most helpless position."[55] Mills also writes:

> He is not aware of having any history, his past being as brief as it is unheroic; he has lived through no golden age he can recall in time of trouble. Perhaps because he does not know where he is going, he is in a frantic hurry; perhaps because he does not know what frightens him, he is paralyzed with fear. This is especially a feature of his political life, where the paralysis results in the most profound apathy of modern times.[56]

The labour movement's work, of course, is to put this right, and provide the middle class with the vital energy that will prevent it from becoming simply a mediocre class. Providing vital energy implies making it into a social force—one that produces its own discourse, and goes beyond exclusively administrative demands to deal with the framework that actually shapes its existence. Labour unions in Quebec, and in many countries including Canada, the United States, France, Germany, Great Britain, Belgium, the Netherlands, and Denmark, have launched campaigns against tax evasion or tax havens.[57] North American labour initiatives have led opposition to sweatshops, and unions have publicized the threat that free-trade agreements pose for public institutions and services. These are efforts to shape an order that will be different from the economic globalization that enables financial and industrial oligarchs to prosper in the secrecy of tax havens, free zones, and duty-free ports.

However, it does not always seem as if these professions of faith, critical approaches, theoretical considerations, and political commitments bring about a real change in union strategies. While laudable, they are essentially marginal, one might even say detached, activities that unions are occasionally willing to undertake on the periphery of their numerous and demanding other responsibilities, such as defending their members' interests on a day-to-day basis or carrying out major negotiations as part of bureaucratic entities that can be as difficult to handle as a government department. The dilemma affecting unions, torn between the general and the particular, between large-scale politics and small-scale management, summarizes the difficulties of the labour movement. The debate is not just a matter of setting priorities. It involves two approaches that are often contradictory, for reflections on the overall framework of life that determines the subjectivity of workers and professionals are likely to lead to conclusions that contradict positions dictated by circumstance and taken in strictly administrative contexts.

A fundamental choice is at issue. Is the labour movement political, and should it remain so, or should it from now on conform to the flabby and strictly managerial rules associated with the word governance? Politics is what happens when people who belong to a community give themselves the capacity to discuss and define the fundamental principles that govern life in society. To act politically therefore implies that we place our discourse and action beyond the social co-ordinates to which we are confined by institutionalized power, and that we discuss all of the rules and mechanisms that require us to be situated here, in this way. We need to be less involved in playing the game of currently prevailing managerial, stock-market, capitalist, and ultraliberal dynamics in the hope of extracting some benefit from them, so that we can put more energy into establishing new formal rules. Governance places union representatives in partnerships that are explicitly recognized as involving unequal players. Subject to the obligation of reaching "consensus," unions are invited to these processes not to genuinely redefine the rules of life in society, but to provide the support of the workers' and professionals' movement to industrial development and projects driven by high finance. In this context, the workers' and professionals' movement, along with representatives of environmental groups, Indigenous peoples, and local residents, are expected to graft onto the great capitalist project a few minor initiatives that can be described to their members as "steps in the right direction," "concessions we were able to obtain," "moral victories," "strategic partnerships," and other trivialities. Governance presents itself once again as an art of private management raised to the status of politics, and whose purpose is to confiscate the political realm.

The political road, of course, is much more difficult, less immediately gratifying, and more uncertain than the path of governance. In this context, it can even be viewed as revolutionary, in the sense that revolution means consigning to the past the institutions of power that are harmful to the common good. But why choose the hostile political road when you can try to move your pawns forward in the spacious, elegant apartments where the game of governance is played? Because—we may recall here the views of Rosa Luxemburg—the game of governance may ultimately become even more painful, psychologically, than the weight of political commitment. The pressure on wages caused by the globalization of work, the closure of factories that are moving away, fiscal avoidance practised proudly and legally, overwork leading to massive prescriptions for psychoactive medications, uncertainty regarding pension plans as a result of erratic stock market movements that lead us to fear the worst, not to mention the pure and simple collapse of industrial organization that could be the outcome of a highly plausible oil and then financial crisis: all of these prospects make the participation of labour groups in the ritual gatherings of governance more problematic and difficult than radical struggle, although the latter is certainly genuinely worrisome in its own right.

The question, then, is to choose between politics or governance: will the labour movement keep on being a part of the capitalist system and its growth, ensuring the system is acceptable to union members and making union funds available to publicly traded companies, or will it be part of a concerted struggle against the system's unjust, damaging, and fatally destructive effects? These questions, fiercely raised in the early twentieth century by Luxemburg in the course of a bitter theoretical and strategic debate with those whom she viewed as social democratic "revisionists"—Eduard Bernstein and Karl Kautsky—may have become unconscious today, but they are still present.

The actors' identities, however, have changed over time. Today we no longer have social democratic ideologues in labour organizations ensuring that members keep on the straight and narrow path of collaboration. Lawyers, possibly without realizing it themselves, are there to do the job. As soon as union members get excited, start to think politically instead of administratively, and present themselves as a social body with sovereign power over its own assets, instantly they appear, armed with their "knowledge" (which is nothing more than the grammar of power), ready to tell people what their rights are and warn them of what will befall if they show the slightest impulse toward independence. They were the ones who blocked every movement toward civil disobedience in 2012 when the time came to fight Bill 78, the work of Quebec's "liberal" government—a "special law," voted during a period of massive student protests, that imposed steep fines on anyone who disrupted class schedules and restricted citizens' right to demonstrate. The bill was denounced by Amnesty International as well as a group of over sixty Quebec law professors, two independent UN experts on freedom of assembly and peaceful association and freedom of opinion and expression, UN High Commissioner for Human Rights Navanethem Pillay, and Quebec's Commission for Human Rights and the Rights of Youth. This is the law that was viewed even by former Quebec premier Jacques Parizeau, who chose his words carefully, as a "fascist temptation." The problem is that labour unions derive their status, and the administrative nature of their existence, from the capitalist state that it is their job to fight. Effective strikes are forbidden by the state under the Orwellian claim of ensuring the "right to strike"—a right that is rigorously circumscribed, following a script that means strikes will generally be avoided and can always be ended by a "special law" or "back-to-work" legislation.

The administrative status of labour unions forces them to think about the economy strictly according to the dogmatic terms of trade and finance, that is, strictly according to the individualistic strategies of each actor, as if each union member should be considered separately. This is to forget the comment of sociologist Gabriel Tarde, who wrote in *Psychologie économique* (1902):

> Sympathetic strikes, the strikes carried out by workers who have no interest in them and who will suffer for them, simply to show solidarity with comrades in whose fate they are interested—these were imagined in America, in the country we have been told is the most utilitarian, the most advanced in terms of economic progress. Nowhere have we seen as many financial sacrifices made for an idea, a question of principle, a feeling of sympathy, as in this country given over to well-understood self-interest.[58]

At the simplest level, labour lawyers remind the advocates of combative unionism of something that was criticized by philosopher Walter Benjamin: the fact that the regime will tolerate the labour movement only as long as it ensures that the framework within which established power is exercised remains intact. In his "Critique of Violence," Benjamin presents the right to strike as a way, for a state governed by the rule of law, to pacify the people that it must control. In no way will it be acceptable for unions to affect the actual working of the regime, whether by a strike or any other means. A revolutionary general strike, for instance, that aims to paralyze the state in order to compel it to carry out radical change, would be viewed as illegal. In the case of simultaneous strikes,

> labor will always appeal to its right to strike, and the state will call this appeal an abuse, since the right to strike was not "so intended," and

take emergency measures. For the state retains the right to determine that a simultaneous use of strike in all industries is illegal, since the specific reasons for strike admitted by legislation cannot be prevalent in every workshop.[59]

Because established authorities will never grant a right that could be used to overthrow them, the workers' movement will be forced to sacrifice some of the advantages granted by the regime to ensure its allegiance, and will have to find new and imaginative ways of mobilizing. If this were to happen, means would be lost, but a much more significant political impact would be the outcome. The labour movement today must choose between undertaking political action, which may weaken it materially, or remaining in a state of political weakness while preserving its administrative strength.

3

CULTURE AND CIVILIZATION

THERE ARE two of them: the psychic economy, originating in our flesh, described by Freud in terms such as "quota" of affect, instinctual "investment," "currency" of meaning, or energy "savings"; and the material economy, made up of small business deals, accounting passions, and sumptuary laws. The second economy erodes the motions and emotions of the first. But despite what you might expect, the psychic economy is the one that comes into play when accumulating financial capital is the issue. The art of earning money is a matter of drives, and, as in every other situation, the monetary medium is mobilized to temper and control psychic passions, reduce them to their simplest expression, make them average, and communicate them once they have been tamed in this way. Psychic expression is affected, in a lasting way, by the monetary medium. And money both serves and uses art to speak of its own nature, as a means of mediating affects in the indescribable splendour of mediocrity.

The psychic economy tries to keep the nervous system at a low level of excitement. Satisfying a need, giving free rein to a drive, letting go of tension—these are ways of reducing the agitation that makes us twitch, blocking the forces that cause our nerves to prickle. These acts of release provide a feeling of fullness that results in pleasure. Through utterance, expression, gesture, or object relations, the subject, as long as she is alive, is looking for strategies that will help her free psychic energy. Copulating, eating, grabbing things—these are forms of psychological deployment grounded in a relationship of the inside to the outside.

It is unusual, however, for release to take place without creating friction or conflict. Ethical systems and laws are authoritative institutions that force the subject to "repress." Depending on culture, this may mean not making love before marriage, not jostling bystanders, or not telling the emperor that he has no clothes. Repression means preventing a psychic expenditure. Whenever this happens, the subject must work to contain a psychic drive that wants to manifest itself. If the subject does express the drive under favourable circumstances, it will be said that she is entering a process of psychic "spending": she "invests" an object of desire through gestures, words, or symbols. Her expression may also be seen as a form of "savings," in the sense that these affects are recorded when the subject stops containing them. The person is doing without—economizing—the psychic work needed to repress these drives, which means there are "savings." Society has allowed her to satisfy a desire without getting in the way.

Other circumstances call for repression. Unfortunately, this is what happens most often: the psyche is constantly repressing things. Over and over, it must contain psychic assaults that have no outlet in socially accepted forms. Such forms are like stereotyped scripts for social life: expressing sorrow that we don't truly feel when an acquaintance dies, congratulating a colleague who has won an insignificant award, saying hello to despised subordinates. Freud calls them "neurotic currency" (*neurotische Währung*).

To be psychically rich, then, is to give yourself the means of expressing, as easily and frequently as possible, your psychological wishes, and, especially, not to be forced to contain them in costly repressive processes. For repression is precisely what causes psychic excitement to rise. Hence the uneasiness, unpleasant feelings, agitation, and general neuroses that afflict poor people, faced by a ruling class that displays complete self-control and by hordes of experts and spokespersons who are characterized by the serenity of their daily lives. For the less fortunate, repression is a high ongoing expense. Repression does not mean expelling from our moral setting, once and for all, an intention that is not allowed to exist within the general economy of our mores; it is an effort that has to be made over and over again, at every moment.

Repression means holding an intention back over a long period, without letting it seep through by way of a slip of the tongue or *acte manqué*, until you are able to negotiate its sublimation into a derived form or to disguise it enough that it can slip out looking different.

Money, in its ordinary meaning of wealth accumulated through a socially recognized system of codification, makes the "work" of repression lighter. It easily justifies the lifting of psychological restrictions. From this point of view, being rich means that you can do without—economize on—acts of repression more often than people who are not very rich. German poet Heinrich Heine, in an anecdote later made famous by Sigmund Freud, tells the story of a Hamburg lottery agent who described his encounter with a famous millionaire: "[Rothschild] treated me quite as his equal—famillionairely."[1] According to Freud, this joke expressed the lower-class person's discomfort when faced with a man of higher social standing. "A rich man's condescension . . . always involves something not quite pleasant for whoever experiences it."[2] But when we turn the proposition around, we also see that wealth is a passport to condescension. This is what Heine's lottery agent is subtly pointing out. Wealth and its attributes enable a person to give free rein to vile attitudes that are redeemed by his condition as a wealthy man. The ostentation of wealth is itself a kind of a currency that transforms the expected rejection into expressions of gratitude. Contempt is respectable.

The powerful person benefits, at every moment, from a savings in terms of the work of repression. Through the contempt that he forces others to experience, he externalizes this work. Psychological efforts, because they are foreign to him, become the lot of "ordinary" people (that is, people who comply with order). It's up to them to show their self-restraint, moderation, perhaps humility, and to be obedient or even respectful. The rich person is then able to freely enjoy the sardonic laughter that wells up when one is able to do without (economize) the pompous moralizing intended for the wretched of the earth. (Surely we need not mention, here, the misogynistic blunders or sexual violence of an Italian press magnate who had become his country's president of council, a former director of the International Monetary Fund, or an American president.) Their demonstrations of power are the ultimate negation of the reality principle, for money, when massively concentrated, destroys any barriers erected by scruples. This is the supreme investment: we will make a great effort in order to rise socially to a level where we are spared all of these psychological efforts.

Money plays a completely different role for those who seek to acquire it as wages. This type of income, far from authorizing moral laxity, is only available as compensation for psychological labour. From the start, money funds a significant form of repression: remaining silent. "Shut up, I'm paying you," is the implicit command that comes with your first paycheque. The fact that money buys silence is so clear that employees who are required to maintain professional secrecy in various areas of activity, such as medicine, law, or politics, receive increased compensation. The repression principle is sometimes spectacularly explicit. A team of investigators was once sent to uncover why so many civil servants in a German government department were falling into depression: the study concluded that they were living in psychological torment because there was too great a discrepancy between what they were officially allowed to disclose and what they knew to be the truth.

Today, in the era of totalitarian management and corporate culture, the command has become more comprehensive: "Smile—I'm paying you. Be personally committed to whatever I ask you to do—I'm paying

you. Call on your personal network to support your professional work—
I'm paying you." The insane idea that "the customer is always right" is
another one of these mottoes, or neurotic currencies, that place extreme
psychological demands on those who are subject to them.

The medium of money, in the transactions that it governs, is an agent
that represses violent affects. Its quantum of ferocity becomes apparent if we imagine ordering a meal in a restaurant, eating it, and leaving
without paying the bill. The violence involved is obvious. What power
of coercion is embodied in this medium that allows us to command others! With money lubricating the relationship, the violence remains but
is still deadly, since money enables us to avoid (economize) it: wealthy
people deny violence while carrying it out; poor people repress it while
submitting themselves to it. In the first case, the wealthy person must
never name it while enjoying the hidden prerogatives it provides; in the
second, the poor person must censor it and internalize its workings. The
principle disintegrates, however, when a lottery agent confronted with
the arrogance of Baron Rothschild makes a joke that shifts awareness in
a flash.

A witticism can enable us to erase a situation and write a new script.
Worthies and dignitaries can be stripped naked and plunged brutally into
farce, as filmmaker Pierre Falardeau does in *Le temps des bouffons*:

All the vultures are there: bosses and bosses' wives, financial barons,
frozen pizza kings, real estate mafiosi. That whole gang of benefactors
of humanity. Stinking carcasses that people raise monuments to, prof-
iteers that people think are philanthropists, poor schmoes—friends of
power—disguised as senile senators, women whose asses are too tight,
little cunts sucking their way to the top, crawling journalists dressed
up as brown-nosing editorialists, shady lawyers dressed up as judges
earning $100,000 a year, ass-lickers who think they're artists. The
whole gang is there: a bunch of chrome-plated, medal-wearing, tie-
wearing, gross, vulgar, and trivial people with their fancy clothes and

high-class jewels. They stink of expensive perfume. They're rich— they're good-looking. They're horribly good-looking with their horrible white teeth and their horrible pink skin. And they're partying.[3]

Humour can quickly become sombre. Strangely, Falardeau's filthy words strengthen our dignity. We think of them, and in fact are saved by them, when we see that global oligarchs consume sumptuary spectacles as wretched as the most banal television program. This is the case whether they are staying with the billionaire Desmarais family in Quebec or visiting Trump's grotesque pseudo-Versailles at Mar-a-Lago. Falardeau's words also help us not to flinch at the astonishing scene in Andreas Pichler's documentary *The Venice Syndrome*,[4] in which tourists are seen literally destroying the foundations of the city of Venice while dressed up in period costume to play ancient nobles at pitiful masked balls.

Falardeau's famous narration in *Le temps des bouffons* does more than just provide a somewhat higher vantage point from which to witness such scenes, with which, unfortunately, we have become quite famillionaire. It also shows us the injustice that occurs when rich and poor despise each other. In pitting vulgarity against vulgarity, Falardeau makes it clear that the poor, when they denounce the discreet charm of the bourgeoisie, often pay a price in depreciating themselves. This is not simply mutual contempt between one person and another, but mutual contempt between a rich person and a poor person, in a situation where the feeling they have in common leads to the poor person's debasement. Even people who appreciate wit may quickly lose their assurance at such a time. Heine's character becomes cruder and less witty when he describes the wealthy, lacking self-awareness because they have been made rotten by wealth, as "Millionarr" (a pun combining the German words for millionaire and fool—*Narr*).[5]

This kind of psychic release is not recommended, for it is simply a way of preparing for new trials. It rarely makes us grow in stature. What is left for the rejects of psychic debt? They can be inventive, funny, subtle, creative—all things that will be eyed jealously by those who have been protected by money, since the beginning of time, from having to develop such qualities. Moneyed people will appropriate, after the fact, the fruits of an attitude developed in resistance to them. They will own intellectual property rights in clothing styles initiated by people whose style once made them marginal; in fine colleges, they will teach transcendent works of literature written by society's rejects, with difficulty, and in anger against them; they will gentrify neighbourhoods that were given a mind and a soul by poor people with time on their hands. And so on. They have the option of purchasing exclusive rights to inventions produced by the richness of spirit of people who faced constraints and had to overcome them. At one degree of removal, their well-developed humour gives them the last laugh—a coarse laugh that rings out as they reduce the forms developed without them to the elements of a commercial game. This is their one and only passion, demonstrating financial power and nothing else.

Opinions of the rich and famous

The sumptuous lifestyles of the rich and famous now reflect the industrial mass culture that they have come to imitate. Hans Magnus Enzensberger observed: "The 'ruling class' has not produced a culture of its own for a long time, nor has it given the slightest indication that it needs anything of the sort."[6] The masters of the game abuse themselves. They take their play-acting seriously, watch themselves in their own movie, feel a child-like excitement at the games played in the stadium they caused to be built, and believe their own lies when they read them in their own newspapers. But just because something is laughable doesn't mean that laughter is the only possible response.

There are no doubt similarly ostentatious mansions in every Western country, but consider the example of the Desmarais family's fake royal palace at Sagard, northeast of Quebec City—a pseudo-Palladian building endowed with a swimming pool, gym, and greenhouse, and surrounded by formal Versailles-style gardens, stables, a golf course, a helipad, forty other buildings, seventy-five square kilometres of land, and thirty-two lakes.

The Desmarais family, one of the wealthiest in Canada,[7] has shaped political life in Quebec, Canada, and France for decades. Their privileged connections with political elites were established by Paul Desmarais Sr., whose role in grooming Canadian prime ministers from both major political parties extended from the 1960s until his death in 2013. (According to Peter C. Newman, "No businessman in Canadian history has ever had more intimate and more extended influence with Canadian prime ministers than Desmarais."[8]) Desmarais Sr. was also instrumental in helping Nicolas Sarkozy come to power in France, according to Sarkozy's own account.[9]

A documentary produced by the Desmarais family in 2008 to depict a birthday party for Paul Desmarais Sr.'s wife, released on YouTube by Anonymous in 2012,[10] shows us that the Desmarais palace is as "uninhabitable" as the strictly homogenized suburban houses Adorno described. But beyond the tasteless aesthetic and monarchical etiquette that the video reveals, Sagard's high-society life embodies an organization of political power that is undefined, but real. Watching prominent politicians, financiers, and cultural figures hovering around the Desmarais couple, we understand:

1. That there is a very real order of power that is not translated into any constitutional form or publicly recognized institution. No election, court, structure, or opposition can formally articulate or frame this self-celebrating power.
2. That this elitist order, a stranger to constitutional forms of power, will assimilate traditionally acknowledged forms of power, as is apparent from the way it receives politicians and other figures associ-

ated with formal institutions. They appear wearing insignia, medals, and decorations granted by lawful institutions, but they find themselves in a setting where hierarchy is established in a completely different way.

3. That this order brings together property owners who can register their assets, or those of the banks and multinationals they control, in accommodating jurisdictions (such as tax havens) in order to carry out operations outside the purview of states governed by the rule of law. In this respect they are sovereigns, but their sovereignty is exercised in private, without any known or recognized formal structure.

4. That the definition and description of these new structures of power largely eludes the traditions of political philosophy and settled forms of constitutional theory on the sovereignty of the state. They require us to define new forms of power and to redefine the terms in our political lexicon that are used to describe the evolution of our world.

5. That this power, silent, encrypted, virtual, and transnational, also eludes the critical theories of political emancipation that see democracy as a dialectic between the official speech of a given power and its polemical refutation by those who are governed and who know that intelligence is shared by all. Here we see that informal but all-powerful agents are paradoxically endowed with the attributes of proletarians: they have no voice, no name, no settled abode, and sometimes no formal membership in the body politic. In the economic sphere, their activities shape the fate of communities and dictate how ideology will influence public policy; legally, however, they are ghosts. Entire sections of their capital vanish offshore, and they often use extraterritorial shell companies and company lawyers, acting as frontmen, to prepare the dirty tricks that affect our real economies.

Owners of offshore sovereignty are in a position to elude the law. They can bypass it as they like in accommodating jurisdictions, while expecting it to fully constrain competitors of inferior social classes. They can also make sure that laws are drafted by their agents, who are members of executive bodies within the state apparatus.

In this nightmare of the Sagard oligarchy, as in other dreams, roles and positions are turned upside down. Those viewed as political antagonists are brought together (Lucien Bouchard and Jean Chrétien); those who head institutions and embody public decisions are demoted to the rank of mere guests (Jean Charest); a citizen without any official power sits on his throne at the very top (Paul Desmarais).

Cultural capital

Like an event at court, the gathering at the Desmarais mansion was intended less to provide the king with an artistic performance than to enable him to give a show. In a temporary performance venue specially built for the occasion and embodying the apotheosis of kitsch, surrounded by politicians, financiers, artists, and courtiers who came to occupy a different rank from the one usually assigned to them in the trompe-l'œil of formal democracy, the oligarch that evening wanted to sing a tragic song—"I would have liked to have been an artist"*—while contemplating not the performance itself but his ability to pay for it. Whatever he sees dancing on stage or bursting forth from a painting is, again, his own capital. The oligarch is not at one with the general public, even when he consumes the same cultural trash. He does a poor job of reproducing the look of the court to which he aspires, but the great financier, press magnate, and oil company administrator is nonetheless satisfied with the sham in which he and his attendants are absorbed. He is all the more satisfied with the performance because it is big, which means, from his point of view, that a serial version of it can be marketed. Such is the mark of his

---

* This is a quote from "Le blues du businessman," a song written by Luc Plamondon and Michel Berger.—CB

power: he can bring an entire community to experience the effects of his bad taste, effects which are deployed, with no possible resistance, under the heading of "culture."

A group of tenors came to Sagard to sing Desmarais's life story: this private performance was the climax of his fantasy. As Paul Desmarais sits in the king's seat, the character Paul Desmarais strides on stage, singing words specially written for the occasion by a well-known lyricist. Suddenly, everything about Desmarais becomes a stage rant: the imperious dissatisfaction that he exhibits as a virtue, the delirious megalomania that functions as a precept. The mediocrity of his relationship to the world becomes a model. As a creator, Desmarais can boast of being the one who chooses the kind of art that the public will view as a reference to be known and quoted. While he cannot be original, he can be the origin.

In an age of technical reproduction of the work of art, sponsors find themselves supporting not just an individual artist, school, or discipline, but the consumer products of a mass industry deeply entwined with other areas in which big capital is active. Decisions about what people should consume determine assembly-line production. This had already been noticed in 1944 by Theodor Adorno and Max Horkheimer in *Dialectic of Enlightenment*:

> Movies and radio need no longer pretend to be art. The truth that they are just business is made into an ideology in order to justify the rubbish they deliberately produce. They call themselves industries; and when their directors' incomes are published, any doubt about the social utility of the finished product is removed.[11]

A few items may escape this process of homogenization—a few works of art may fail to comply with the prevailing aesthetic—but this will be done more to satisfy the principle of small differences for a small number of distinguished consumers than to bring about radical change in the system. As Adorno and Horkheimer point out, "Whenever Orson Welles offends against the tricks of the trade, he is forgiven because departures from the norm are regarded as calculated mutations which serve all the more strongly to confirm the validity of the system."[12] Essentially, cultural "goods" serve to shape the mass of individuals who make up the pool of clients and supporters that capital needs. Philosopher Herbert Marcuse restated this argument in *One-Dimensional Man* (1964):

> If the worker and his boss enjoy the same television program and visit the same resort places, if the typist is as attractively made up as the daughter of her employer, if the Negro owns a Cadillac, if they all read the same newspaper, then this assimilation indicates not the disappearance of classes, but the extent to which the needs and satisfactions that serve the preservation of the Establishment are shared by the underlying population.[13]

The cultural landscape that Marcuse describes presents itself as a formal and symbolic apparatus leading people managed and dominated by liberal regimes to channel their psychic energy into a social structure that was there before them—a structure designed and implemented by the dominant class. Expressions of desire and deep-rooted drives are encoded, on the basis of stereotypes, in movies, songs, advertising, and the mass media. While such an explanation may not be sufficient, and while the reduction of the "cultural industry" to an aspect of totalitarian life cannot encompass the reality of all artistic works, this approach does flawlessly embody the attitude of financial investors to works of art—and the way in which capital holders intend to force artists to submit.

Artists don't count

We can now better understand why artists are enjoined to work according to market goals rather than the goals associated with their own creative process. To be an artist/manager or a manager/artist, that is the question. Wealthy "philanthropists," however, are not stumped by such pointless dilemmas: in relation to money, there is only one knowledge, and that is the knowledge held by those who know how to accumulate it. We love art, and on top of that we even care about artists—you can't expect us to actually consider what they think of the economy. It's up to them to adapt. And in paying for art (while enjoying themselves at artists' expense), funders see themselves as the true creators, since they alone make art possible. Not only do they fund it, but they exhaust themselves by working as board members to manage all of its structures.

The artists appreciated by investors are now trying to be "creators" in the investors' own language. Céline Dion and the Cirque du Soleil are thought to have achieved international "success" not according to aesthetic criteria, but in terms of their business plan. Such artists no longer merely provide the labour power that will produce cultural commodities. In a burst of enthusiasm for alienation, or leadership, as we say in management-speak, they are now expected to manage the institutions that exploit them. Entrepreneurship is the criterion setting apart those who are ready to go on to the real thing: creation, no doubt, but by that we mean creation of revenue, surplus value, a business, or jobs.

With full confidence in their own cultural capital, sponsors now have their own schools in which their chosen artists can be trained. Teaching provided in business schools will help converts to cultural governance understand that they should ignore anything said or thought in circles foreign to those into which they are being inducted. A 2014 syllabus from an arts and culture management program illustrates our point: "It is important that arts and culture managers should have at least a basic knowledge of cultural policies. They must be able to go beyond the preconceived ideas and demands traditionally expressed by the arts community." Given its "characteristics," the arts community does, of course, pose "a very special challenge" to enlightened managers, "because of the nature of the product that it provides (cultural works), the characteristics of the people at the heart of its productions (artists), and the meaning of these productions (performances, works of art or symbolic goods) to the people who ask for them," to quote from another syllabus from the same institution. Artists are incorrigible. They tend to take their commitment more seriously than the institutions carrying out the marketing on which their work depends. They therefore have to be taught proper manners in school: how to seduce partners not by the methods to which they have so far been confined (blobs of paint, purple prose, or other such antics), but by finding the business arguments that will convince a big company to put its brand right on the wrapping paper of their artworks. They must learn not only to tolerate this situation, but also to want it. They will give up the naive belief that asset holders should contribute to the arts by paying taxes. The business school, whose board of directors may well be chaired by a member of the oligarchy, will make sure that these ideas are expressed in a kind of business poetry best suited to the system's pretenses, with courses focusing on "management decisions" related to "the economic analysis of cultural industries."

The social pressure to go this way is now very strong. Once converted to business school principles, any self-respecting entrepreneur/ artist will hold forth on "organizational culture, governance, resource allocation, relations between artists and managers, and power dynamics within and around these organizations," and will view fashionable "experiential" approaches as a key way to exercise power. In Quebec, 101 of these "artists" publicly supported the political ambitions of someone who funded their production—a press magnate who can only be viewed as the gravedigger of culture, judging by the bad taste his publications display. But that doesn't matter. Works become products, artists are "cultural sector human resources," audiences are "consumers" and "clients," and they are all part of an "industry" that is intimately connected to the hotel and restaurant, marketing, and supply of materials businesses. The Quebec government's 1992 cultural policy stated that "the development of cultural industries is based on both creative excellence and the ability of businesses to compete."[14] The vocabulary of "cultural management consultancy organizations" providing "cultural mentoring" cannot even be denounced in their own terms: these new practices guarantee "excellence" without anyone asking how that might be critically understood.

Some artists are playing the game, which means they are participating in a new kind of circus. Reinventing, extending, and consolidating a new art of fiction, they come to believe that the profits of a cultural company that "participates in the economy" are more meaningful than its aesthetic concepts. For whatever these aesthetic concepts may be, they will eventually be accepted by audiences targeted by well-designed promotional campaigns.

According to the pure logic of governance, which says that all must adapt and be subordinate to business methods, arts councils and the various ministries that are "competent" in this area become the "partners" of big companies and offer them tax incentives to "invest in culture." Art that is subject to this approach becomes a force ensuring political uniformity, sociological management, and industrial production. Or, to quote the terms used by the "business creators"[15] of the Board of Trade of Metropolitan Montreal, we might say that art is "a generator of quality of life for all Montrealers," a tool for tax or estate planning, and a source of "direct benefits of close to $8 billion, or 6% of our city's GDP."[16] This was in 2011. Adorno and Horkheimer's critique did not go this far.

Artists who do not submit to being trained in this way simply do not count. When someone is too whimsical to acknowledge the authority of numbers, why pay her any attention? What is to be done with someone likely to quote Stéphane Mallarmé, a poet who lost his faith just because a company ruined a few investors in the Panama scandal? "The inability of figures, however grandiloquent, to translate, here arises out of a case; one searches, with this hint that, if a number increases and backs up toward the improbable, it inscribes more and more zeros: signifying that its total is spiritually equal to nothing, almost."[17] Above all, the artist without entrepreneurial training should never be allowed to go near financial records, or even to have an idea of what they might contain. She might then develop an improper interest in ploys that are a little too obvious, pretenses that go a little too far, or counterfeits designed to create emotion. She might find that some elements in the field of finance and administration are actually within her purview as an aesthetic person: the staging of economic rationality, the fiction of expertise, the identification of investors with market protagonists, the dramatic illusion giving rise to pity and terror.

This is easily understood when we consider how big capital stages a daily performance, whether through an iconography that has now been adopted even by the austere *Wall Street Journal*—dynamically blurred photographs illustrating the hyperactivity of businessmen, falsely convincing graphs—or through fawning biographies that echo every poetic nuance of the coming-of-age novel. Investors, executives, and retailers pose at galas that often turn into contests in sycophancy. Generally accepted units of meaning such as "trust," "risk," "crisis," or the priceless "leadership" relentlessly populate financial press headlines, giving rise to narrative considerations derived from the aesthetics of film, drama, and novels. The jargon we are being fed today on governance and innovation is all part of the same farce. According to this script, a mysterious realm of knowledge encompasses the economy and management of world affairs. Investors, in fact, would like artists to take their turn as a docile audience applauding their sleight of hand.

They don't always get what they want. How many undefeated artists have realized that board-appointed experts have no understanding of their institution's issues, and that the insubordination of underpaid staff is the only glue holding the whole thing together? The artists soon understand that there is no such thing as an ability to manage independently of practice, any more than there is an art of communicating or a marketing technique that you could learn at the university and that would work even with no specific idea of the contents to be communicated. The ideology of management, when applied, can lead to disaster: What idiocies do we not hear in the name of innovation, development, transformation, entrepreneurship, and profitability? We know of artists enjoined, by experts suddenly appointed to run their organization, to invest in real estate—a move that would certainly have ruined them had they carried it out. Others have had to deal with "innovative" proposals that require them to completely change their purpose to take up some new activity improbably defined as a "growth area." Often, incompetent administrators have loudly blamed resistant artists for "defying authority," with subsequent decisions usually demonstrating that the artists' resistance was completely justified.

In some cases, when the artists are convinced they are faced with someone who knows more than they do, they may ask their teachers very simple questions that go to the heart of the matter. Gertrude Stein, writer and art collector, obsessively questioned the nature of money ("Is money money or isn't money money"[18]) as she sought to distinguish money that is diverted, money that is accumulated, and money that circulates in a world perceptible to the senses. Sculptor and visual artist Joseph Beuys asked the same basic question, which became the title of his book: "What is money?"[19] Beuys's premise, according to which everyone must be an artist if we want to create a society in which money generates fair relationships, completely subverts established hierarchies. For if we admit that we are all artists, then businesspeople must admit that the instruments devised by finance are to a large extent works of fiction, while artists must acknowledge that they can take charge of management and think about the economy, using the tools that art puts at their disposal.

This is actually what government officials and businesspeople implicitly recognize when they tell artists that "they too" must get to work, in the right manner and following the right advice. After all, what is so special about business "expertise," if its key elements can be grasped through programmed interactions with a "mentor" or by following a "microprogram" devised by a business school? What is the profound wisdom of a corpus that even artists, thought to be on the lowest rung in terms of business savvy, could so easily assimilate? This is actually a very strange position. What if such knowledge were not anyone's exclusive preserve, and what if there were an art of administration irreducible to the skills of any particular social category? And what if there were not a specifically artistic way of managing things, but an aesthetic approach to the economy that would put the idea of the economy back in the field of plurality, intelligence, and the world as perceived by the senses? In 1936, the impetuous dramatist Antonin Artaud, deeply distressed by income inequalities, boldly asserted a highly reasonable principle: "Decongesting the Economy means simplifying it, filtering what is superfluous, for hunger cannot wait."[20]

What if we were to understand, also, that literature and the arts often put the economy back into the various disciplines to which this idea belongs, whatever its origin may be? Reading André Gide's novel *The Counterfeiters*, we are reminded that before using the word "ecology," scientists referred to "the economy of nature." Gide tells us that nature, whose "spectacle" reflects the astounding diversity of its laws, seems to have tried "one after the other every possible manner of living and moving,"[21] leading to the exclamation: "What economy has enabled some forms to survive!"[22] This expression resonates with the meaning given to the word economy by an eighteenth-century English naturalist, Gilbert White of Selborne. From White's perspective, when cows cooling off in a pond happen to provide sustenance for fish because the dung they drop into the water is full of insects, this is the economy of nature organizing itself.[23] We also hear echoes of Jean-Joseph Menuret, the eighteenth-century biologist who wrote an article in the *Encyclopédie* (1751) on "Œconomie animale."

In the first poem of *Fureur et mystère*, René Char breaks the silence to write: "To exceed the economy of creation, to increase the blood of gestures, task of all light."[24] Reading this, we hear the intrinsic bond between the economy and ancient and extensive forms of organization.

Studies of the theological argument about images in Byzantium indicate the nature of this bond: they describe a relationship of mutual dependence between images and symbols, with the first deriving their power from transcendent references, and the second owing their existence to the mediation of images.[25] Once it was launched, the term "economy" found itself at the heart of writing in many disciplines, from the sociology of Gabriel Tarde to the linguistic theories of Algirdas Julien Greimas, the literary criticism of Gérard Genette, and the philosophy of Hermann Lotze. What can we learn from these linked usages opened up by aesthetics? That the economy is not the business of economists. That it deals, overall, with expected and fruitful relations between elements that it establishes as interconnected. Whatever the area involved, the economy does not belong to any given specialty, as evidenced by the use of the word in all cultural practices and fields of knowledge.

This radical critique of the economy leads to far more than a simple alternative reinterpretation of the dogmas produced by those who proclaim themselves the owners of the economy's specific meaning. It helps us understand how official "economists," true bankers of meaning, imprison thought within the narrow confines of their discipline; a hyperactive overuse of concepts, models, and associations of ideas is one way of achieving this. In 1876, philosopher and biologist Richard Avenarius published a book entitled *Philosophy as a Way of Thinking About the World According to the Principle of the Smallest Amount of Force*[26] (a literal translation of the German title), in which he describes the act of thinking as a way of cutting singular and specific operations short in order to conserve physiological resources. Thinking is costly, from a biological point of view, and the body needs to economize on mental operations. To do so, thought provides itself with what Avenarius describes as "statements" (*Aussagen*), which are designed to neutralize the meaning of specific events, or things in a state of constant flux, by opposing to them standard schemata that take the place of thought responsive to context.

The value of "statements" is that they are suited to a wide variety of situations, to which they can be adapted with a minimum degree of invest-ment. This use of statements is what economic "science" enacts to an optimal and excessive extent. The goal is to incorporate, into an indepen-dent model, what we already have in common on the basis of everything that already exists. The principle of economic stability, in the biological sense of the word "economic," is to reduce, to the greatest extent pos-sible, the expenditure involved in the work of adapting to change. This explains why those who present themselves as economic experts have so little capacity to envision the thing in itself, the thing that can be per-ceived by the senses, the exception, or the unusual: anything that cannot be incorporated into their blind model is rejected as pointless or possibly even dangerous. What is economic, in Avenarius's sense, is the apparatus that makes it possible to incorporate, with the least effort, any outside change and any individuality, to the benefit of a system—economic "sci-ence"—that has become destructive, by reason of its very structure, of everything it does not understand. Surely the field that has appropriated the name of "economics" can survive on a regional basis, and, we would hope, take the form of open debates, as a discipline analyzing production, accounting, and exchange of goods—but, ideally, under one of the differ-ent names given to it in the past, whether chrematistics, physiocracy, or econometrics.

Art, meanwhile, reminds us that there is no such thing as a specific art of economic thinking. Each of us fashions a deliberate way of managing that keeps us on good terms with otherness. Such is the power to which aesthetics brings us back. The very meaning of the economy is at stake.

Portrait of the artist as a social worker

Like the expert, the artist subject to the restrictions of private manage-ment can be drafted into service in times of crisis. While the expert tries to reassure us by making the unforgivable and the scandalous appear necessary and rational, the artist is called to the victims' bedside to depoliticize the event through multiple benefit concerts and declarations of support. She is assigned the role of social worker of our collective life. Constrained by the blackmail of the powerful, the artist is strongly encouraged to appear in public at the slightest disaster; free publicity is viewed as sufficient compensation. This is what happened following the Lac-Mégantic tragedy of July 6, 2013. That night, a train full of crude oil blew up in people's faces; forty-seven people died in a fire that destroyed the centre of a small Quebec town. Companies involved in rail transportation were undeniably responsible, given their negligence and avarice. And yet the population, overwhelmed and heartbroken, did not rise up in anger or radically challenge a model that had once again demonstrated its destructive potential. Artists were called in precisely for the purpose of rescuing companies and governments by making sure that no one went beyond the management of feelings. Above all, we must avoid cultivating such feelings from a critical perspective.

What happened at Lac-Mégantic was not an accident. Around 11 p.m. on July 5, a fire was reported in the lead locomotive of the train that was destined to explode. To stop the engine, which had been operating without any human presence, firefighters unknowingly disabled the air brake system. The train, badly parked, poorly secured, and left unattended, began its crazy downhill journey shortly before 1 a.m. on July 6. In its investigation report, the Transportation Safety Board of Canada (TSB) noted that the Montreal, Maine and Atlantic (MMA) railway company had a "weak safety culture" that "contributed to the continuation of unsafe conditions and unsafe practices," that there were "significant gaps between the company's operating instructions and how work was done day to day," and that "employee training, testing, and supervision were not sufficient, particularly when it came to the operation of hand brakes and the securement of trains." The TSB report also stated that Transport Canada had been aware for several years that MMA should be inspected more often because it presented a high level of risk, but government officials "did not always follow up" to make sure problems had been corrected, and had waited eight years to audit the company's safety management system even though inspections clearly indicated the system was not effective.[27] In other words, the explosion of the tank cars that careened into Lac-Mégantic, each one loaded with 131,000 litres of highly flammable petroleum[28] of a type incorrectly identified[29] by incompetent or cynical managers, was in no way an "accident" (*Merriam-Webster's Unabridged*: "an event or condition occurring by chance or arising from unknown or remote causes"): it was a disaster waiting to happen. (And such incidents are not all that rare: in 2016, there were over a thousand railway "accidents" in Canada, and almost eleven thousand in the United States.[30])

To increase its profit margins, the MMA had reduced to a minimum its investments in safety, thus externalizing disaster risk and exposing the communities adjacent to its railway routes to severe problems. The TSB notes that about six million litres of oil were released from the tank cars.[31] In 2012, Transport Canada had granted the MMA special permission to assign a single engineer to its trains:[32] Was this due to lobbying? corruption? The Quebec government was certainly aware of this transportation activity but never opposed it. According to an environmental advocacy group, the Société pour vaincre la pollution (SVP), high amounts of carcinogenic products found their way into the area's water system; the organization's 2013 study showed a rate of carcinogenic polycyclic aromatic hydrocarbons that was 394,444 times the Quebec standard for surface waters.[33] Approximately 100,000 litres of oil flowed into Lake Mégantic, upstream from the Chaudière River; as a consequence, the site is now a source of pollution throughout other areas in Quebec.

Artists, called in by authorities to divert attention from the crime, went in as a group to support a deeply shaken community. A huge outdoor stage was set up to welcome a host of star performers imported from Montreal. Sponsors made room for themselves, as well: the unfortunate people of Lac-Mégantic spent the entire summer with a prominent Loto-

Québec sign in their faces. In a state of shock, artists responded from the heart, but they did not yet have the critical distance to ask: Am I being manipulated? What is my role within a system that hires me to comfort victims of a disaster for which this system is responsible? By rushing to help a population that supposedly only wants to be comforted, am I not legitimizing the claim that this was simply an accident? Is my art no more than an anaesthetic? Should my performance serve to isolate emotions and accentuate their release as people turn away from any object associated with the situation? Crisis management experts took advantage of artists' generosity, whose support gave them a head start in organizing state catharsis. Paul McCartney himself, epitomizing virtue, invited survivors and distressed community members to see him perform in Quebec City. Lac-Mégantic was now something you might read about in *People* magazine. Suddenly, the story was no longer political: it was all about feeling the right feelings. For those in power, there was no wrong note.

In any case, a poignant dramatic tableau was needed for posterity. In the era of "artistic capitalism" described by Gilles Lipovetsky and Jean Serroy in their recent book, *L'esthétisation du monde*, our system has completely incorporated artistic practices, to the point of giving them importance under all circumstances.

> The more art seeps into daily life and the economy, the less it is charged with a high spiritual value; as the aesthetic dimension becomes widespread, more and more it appears as one of life's simple occupations, an accessory with no other purpose than to decorate ordinary life and make it livelier and more sensual.[34]

There are no scruples involved. The destruction of Lac-Mégantic's core was the opportunity for the Quebec government to plan the reconstruction, unilaterally, of an area whose residents were in shock. Power can show good taste, even when times are hard. The memory of the disaster will now be a performance. The crime scene will be covered with a "memorial park" designed for tourists and complemented by an adjacent shopping area. An online representation of "*Lac-Mégantic après...*" (Lac-Mégantic afterwards) shows the instrumental and strategic role played by aesthetics in managing the crisis through public manipulation. Three months after the disaster, the town was expected to welcome five thousand tourists coming to view the debris. Now that "beauty" is everywhere, and since taste is viewed as a completely subjective matter and anything can be turned into a saleable commodity, the devastated landscape at the heart of Lac-Mégantic can support a lucrative voyeuristic business with full camera coverage.

To facilitate the transition, Bill 57, hastily voted by the Quebec government to plan the reorganization of the area, threatened to expropriate the homes of many citizens even though their houses had been spared. First, they were invited to move of their own accord, selling their houses at a discount to building contractors who would benefit from reconstruction contracts. At a time when corruption issues in the building industry have become a media soap opera, you can't help but wonder about this. The government created an exceptional situation for the Lac-Mégantic community after the explosion, assigning full powers to public authorities. City council's term of office was extended, the public call for tenders process was bypassed, and the power to transfer businesses and expropriate residents became fully arbitrary. The amount of the prize was sixty million dollars, and eventually, a private contract was awarded to Pomerleau to clean up the site and characterize the soils. This company had been cited in March 2013 by a witness at the Charbonneau Commission—a public inquiry, chaired by Justice France Charbonneau, into corruption in the awarding of public construction contracts in Quebec and the use of straw men to channel illegal funds to political parties. Pomerleau was also given the job of planning the various stages of railway reconstruction. By October 2013, some employees of subcontracting firms were claiming that they had been asked to work more slowly, or even to undo what had just been done, in order to slow down contract execution.[35]

A dislocated relationship to reality

But who really remembers Lac-Mégantic? Like other "major events," these "historic moments" that we experience live on TV tend to vanish as soon as they have been consumed. In his essay *Die Antiquiertheit des Menschen*, written in 1956, German philosopher Günther Anders had already identified television as harmful to a community's relationship with reality. Even those most resistant to this medium are affected by it: when someone leaves home to spend time with her fellow human beings, she realizes that the people she is counting on to make "reality" exist, in a social sense, have stayed home to watch an imitation of social reality on television. Far from being a mass media, television is, on the contrary, a demassification force. It separates and isolates the subjects that make up the collectivity while offering everyone the same thing at the same time. We coexist socially in sharing a reality that we consume only in isolation. Television thus generates a new sociological being, the mass hermit. "Millions of them, simultaneously cut off from and yet identical to each other, sit secluded in their homes—not to renounce the world but rather to make absolutely sure they don't miss even a single instant of the world's image they see on the screen."[36] Reality is dressed up, cut up, framed, and formatted, and television delivers it to our homes like a commodity so that we do not need to live it or carry it out.

Television enables us not to live something that is happening at a distance, but to deny that the distance exists. It does not establish a relation with something great and deep happening independently of it; rather, it seems to completely contain what it presents. Paradoxically, what television denies is the remoteness of what it conveys. The first reason for this is that the screen presents itself not as a reproduction of the world, but as a window on it. Anders insists that it does not compose its image based on (*nach*) the world: it absolutely replaces the world. This means that in the end, we will genuinely not know the difference between attending an event through the media and physically participating in it. A second reason is that programmers have succeeded in getting TV personalities to produce relationships of pseudo-intimacy with their audience.

> When I turn on my TV and see the president, even though he is thousands of miles away, suddenly, there he is, sitting in my living room to chat with me. . . . When the television announcer appears on screen, with calculatedly spontaneous affection, she shares profound insights with me, as if there were something between us. . . . Whether as familiar or indiscreet visitors, they come to me "pre-familiarized."[37]

In this way, the power granted by the medium—being able to follow an event at a distance, being able to know what other people are thinking without talking to them—becomes an obligation: to stay home from events, to stop creating them through the joint presence of those attending them, to stop engaging in conversation with others. Authorized "events" are those organized by television, with extras provided as needed.

This fragmentation is ideal for business, since it enables merchants to present, through television channels, products that take the emotional place of the social bond that the medium precludes.

The mediocratic regime is bringing its full weight to bear. If we want to criticize it in a way that will be heard beyond our insiders' groups, we will have to try to use its language—on television, in particular. The noxious magic of this medium, according to Anders, derives from the fact that it presents a world that has already been analyzed, statements that have already been thought out. Television "glosses over the fact that it presents a judgment that has already been pronounced. . . . In order to persuade the consumer that they are not being persuaded to believe anything, the judgement-turned-picture abandons the appearance of being a judgement."[38] In terms of thought, the screen does not claim to give us something that has been developed intellectually. It provides us with a result, an already grasped truth, without requiring us to go through the stages that have enabled it to exist; this is baby food for the mind. This is why it is so difficult for anyone appearing on television to try to think. The experience is violent for all concerned, like being told to swallow a whole raw potato instead of a spoonful of mash.

Television may sometimes be used in an attempt to surprise people, the goal, of course, being always to convey thought. However, you can only do that if you are able to get on TV. And as Chomsky has pointed out, television always wins in that it only gives you a very short time in which to speak. It becomes a receptacle for clichés, the perfect setting for a yelling match. Any paradoxical, reflective remark will be spit out like the pit of a fruit. Such is the desperate predicament faced by intellectuals who try to use this formidable amplifier of their voice: exposure, which is the only way of reaching hundreds of thousands of people, can only be achieved through overexposure that will burn you up. Nothing you tried to say will remain, except, perhaps—and this is what you are gambling on—a doubt, which will cause some people (or maybe even many) to go further, beyond the relationship to the image.

Subversidized art

A number of artists, such as Dries Verhoeven, deplore the fact that in recent times, the institutionalization of art has discouraged many artists from being subversive. The works of these artists, the argument goes, are standardized to satisfy the expectations of ministries of culture, museums, and other academies. Verhoeven sought to put the situation right through a dramatic performance, *Ceci n'est pas . . .* , presented in downtown Montreal in the spring of 2015 for ten consecutive days. The work was intended to be shocking and provocative. In a square cage barely two square metres in size, a performance, which changed every day, was designed to attract onlookers' attention. For hours, a soldier repeatedly destroyed his drum; a Black hockey player performed contortions with a chain around his foot as if he were a circus animal; a seductive female dwarf tried to pick people up in a bar; a father, almost completely naked, read a story to his little girl, who sat on his lap in her underwear. We also saw an unmarried mother, and a Canadian miner carrying out exploitation in the South. The cage was transparent, and yet it was not. It really did hold human beings. To see a human being in a cage is not insignificant: the cage was truly part of the performance. What happened in the cage did not happen in the same way as in ordinary performances. We could only see the soldier, the Black man, the dwarf, the little girl, the unmarried mother, and the miner as caged beings, even though most of the *tableaux vivants* seemed intended to include the "fourth wall" (or maybe even four "fourth walls"?).

This was subversive. Be aware that shocking things are happening here! On the first day, there was even a legend explaining how subversive it all was. There is a paradox, however. This revival of shocking art, intended to outwit institutionalized forms, was itself subsidized. Included in the Festival TransAmériques, which is funded by government departments and agencies, the hotel industry, and the mainstream media, this officially subversive work was announced as such and was taken very seriously. The goal was to be subversive, but within the boundaries determined by the institutions of subsidized art. The "subversive" nature of the act was manifest, as if it had been officially certified as such by Ministry of Culture officials. This is full-scale institutionalization. Verhoeven's work is a replay of once provocative scenes created by Judith Malina and Julian Beck back in the days when the Living Theatre surprised New Yorkers in the street; the banality of his institutionalized derangement is as familiar as Duchamp's urinal.

Every well-known taboo was represented: the working-class soldier destroying his drum like a Luddite, the popularity of Black athletes in circus games reminiscent of colonial exhibitions, the almost naked father and young child reading a story together in a healthy psychological balance a hair's breadth away from incest and pedophilia, the seductively dressed dwarf revealing the discriminatory history of sexuality. "Subversion" proceeds through signalling, and if one does not understand what is being denounced in broad terms, everything will be made explicit through an explanatory legend or a song conveying the message: the struggle against racism, denouncing Canadian foreign policy, the need for physical contact between father and daughter, the right to be different in a context of seduction, and so on. We are well within the limits of what this subversidized art can admit and understand: a series of clichés that are found every day in mass-circulation newspapers, government publications, and television variety shows.

Subversidized art is genuinely shocking. But that does not mean that it acts on the audience in a subversive manner. We may be disturbed by bad taste, impudence, provocation, or insult, but in fact, it is our intelligence that is being attacked: it is hard to believe that an artist still expects to shock us with such dated tricks. What we see in the glass cage is the shallow repetition of a tired gesture. As a passerby remarked from a distance: "I didn't bother to look because we're right next to the museum of contemporary art, so I'm pretty sure it must be 'contemporary art.'" At this point, we know the song.

These stereotypes of remote-controlled subversion also have a deeper, more disturbing effect. We are disgusted and do not immediately understand why. Is it because they look like a bad student joke? Is it the artist's lack of courage? the feeling of déjà vu? The answer is probably to be found in the dangerous proximity of subversion and perversion, brilliantly analyzed by philosopher Mikel Dufrenne in a 1977 book whose title juxtaposes those two words.[39] The slightest wrong move leads from one to the other, and the idea of "subversion" then justifies crude expressions of a perverse pleasure that is denounced, but only at a superficial level. This is what television does when it obsessively displays the sensational images of an atrocious murder or a degrading brawl that it claims to be denouncing.

The scenes thrown in our faces in downtown Montreal to force us to confront our so-called taboos, putting actors in a glass cube—including a little girl wearing a tiny bra, who was certainly not old enough to give her consent to this collaboration, who was filmed all day long by idiotic onlookers, and who had nothing to do except be distracted by the exclamations of women denouncing her participation—these scenes create a perverse moment out of nothing. Displaying pedophilia, reducing a Black man to a circus animal, exhibiting a dwarf in an outfit that is supposed to be what all women aspire to (even though feminism has denounced this reductiveness for decades), stigmatizing a young pregnant woman, this is what *Ceci n'est pas . . .* took pleasure in doing, under the pretext of exposing an unease for which the unfortunate audience was supposed to feel guilty. All of this in the name of emancipation from cultural institutions—but this obligatory process simply revealed, once again, their negligence.

A cardboard vision of the world

Others show greater tact. Visual artist Mitch Mitchell unsettles us in a productive way by working on small cardboard containers. Hundreds of these simple but highly meaningful objects are stacked or piled up in a big room where we can see them from above as we move around. We are offered a significant point of view on the gigantic industry involved in moving commodities: not our point of view, but the point of view of the financial actors and technicians who manage this huge worldwide enterprise. Cargo shipping and commodity overproduction suddenly leave the abstract world, in which they appear irrational and bearable, and present themselves in their unbelievable and megalomaniac proliferation. Miniature containers, scattered by the hundreds in the Sporobole exhibition space in Sherbrooke, Quebec, embody three major stages in a container's life. First, Mitchell shows us infinite vistas of stacked containers in a vast random arrangement. Then, he reproduces the moment they are loaded onto various transport vehicles. Finally, he shows us their last location, a landfill where they are massively piled up in a shapeless mass. By providing us with a view from above—we are like giants in the middle of what seem to be tiny boxes that may easily be crushed in passing—the installation puts us in the position of a manager who sees this deployment strictly in accounting terms. Each element, in itself, becomes derisory. The cardboard of which each unit is made reinforces the impression of insignificance. As we leave the exhibition, Mitchell provides us with a pattern enabling each of us to create our own unit. The artist overcomes the classic tension between aesthetics and business by using aesthetics to signify the overall vision that prevails in the world of business.

The managerial point of view can also lead to critical meditation. The exhibition leads us to notice this. Sharing the ideology's point of view is a way for us to try and overthrow it. The revolution is not spectacular. When the overall vision is reduced to the accounting dimension, the social, political, and economic repercussions of industrial deployment are concealed; but if the work embodies a vision open to political questions, it helps us make connections that no individual, thinking in isolation, could grasp. Steel shipping containers carry more than goods and trinkets manufactured by people who are slaves in the East for people with purchasing power in the West. They bring Colombian cocaine to New York through discreet channels in Trinidad and Tobago, or weapons from the former Soviet Union to Angola, and they may also resonate with the cries of clandestine migrants travelling from Morocco through Portugal to the waters of the St. Lawrence. These shipping containers both visibly display crude realities and shroud them in silence and darkness: they are black boxes, surrounded by the debris of human suffering, that no one wants to discover or listen to. Managed by import/export companies registered in tax havens, they are carried by freighters registered in free ports and filled with products manufactured in the sweatshops of free zones. The dolls, plastic chairs, and bulbs of garlic they bring us are a symptom of what we choose to leave unsaid regarding the industries that exploit labour today as if we were still in the nineteenth century. Containers show what goes on behind the scenes of commodity fetishism and its fiction of self-produced goods.

To what reality do the tales contained in these black boxes refer? Over the past few years, a focus on containers has come from art. Because they are silent about what they reveal, containers shock and impress us. Photographers often use surprising perspectives to show them to us. We gasp when we see tens of thousands of them occupying monotonous industrial fields, in the suburbs of metropolises where fetishized commodities are deployed. Andreas Gursky has photographed such landscapes. Edward Burtynsky suggests their cold heaviness with his photographs of northern industrial ports. A German theatre festival, Politik im Freien Theater, used them as an illustration in 2005. Photographer Chris Jordan provides astonishing images of containers piled up in ordinary landfills on the west coast of the United States. In 2005, there were more than one million abandoned containers surrounding American ports. Investors, sensing a business opportunity, have transformed them into units to be used as homes, or possibly jails. Artists of other kinds, also inspired by their potential for reuse, are suddenly coming up with unusual recycling proposals to humanize them. Japanese architect Shigeru Ban has even designed residential units based on containers—a project of genuine aesthetic merit. Some have specialized in using them on stage. Other examples may be found online[40] of transformations so effective that we risk forgetting the dark reality of the economy that these proposed uses subvert. Containers are given new life, not so that we can forget where they come from, but to add, to the tales of horror they embody, an episode that might redeem their meaning and a hope that one day the macabre system that has made them possible will be a thing of the past.

4

REVOLUTION:
ENDING WHAT HARMS
THE COMMON GOOD

W HEN he accepted the Nobel Prize for Literature in 1957, Albert Camus reflected on the times he was living in:

> Today everything is changed and even silence has dangerous implications. The moment that abstaining from choice is itself looked upon as a choice and punished or praised as such, the artist is willy-nilly impressed into service. "Impressed" seems to me a more accurate term in this connection than "committed." Instead of signing up, indeed, for voluntary service, the artist does his compulsory service. Every artist today is embarked on the contemporary slave galley.[1]

Like any artist, we are born in a turbulent sea, forcibly embarked.

But when knowledge is expertly produced to conform to ideology, everything conspires to deny the condition we are in. The way we manage our knowledge of the present is supposed to guarantee our belief that everything is under control. Knowledge—the only kind that counts because it is funded, and recognized by peers and acolytes—supports the empirical realm. This official knowledge assigns meaning to power structures according to the expectations of the powerful, that is, its funders. It makes structures into facts of nature, providing the semantic mortar to organize and support institutions of authority in our minds. Everything is done to avoid a break in tone, except in the utopian dreams of intellectuals who have lost their way. And yet, embarking on politics is still a logical necessity. Collectively, we still cannot help engaging in anxious and ill-mannered reflections on our society, even though we may believe that this type of expression has now been permanently confined to the marginal realm of criticism.

Rosa Luxemburg, a Marxist writer active at the turn of the twentieth century, aptly pointed out that people do not become revolutionaries because they love crisis or catastrophe, but because they fear the crisis and catastrophe to which the established system of our time is leading us. Luxemburg reminded everyone that the capitalist economy was headed for disaster and was bringing disaster to the peoples subject to its regime; for this reason, political will, among other things, was needed to bring it down.[2] In Luxemburg's time, there was a strong belief that Marx's predictions, which Engels had done everything in his power to present as "scientific" (positivist), were true: predictions that capitalism was destined to collapse from its own contradictions and that revolutionary force was needed only to help it fall.

Luxemburg's uncompromising stance has now dissolved into other approaches that involve no more than coping with capital's apparently unshakable power. Social democracy, or social liberalism, has meant safeguarding structures of production and financialized capital, while fighting to lessen the exploitation of the workers and employees who make the system work. In some cases, it has also meant saving capital itself from its propensity for crisis, by absorbing the consequences unleashed by sorcerers' apprentices in private management.

Helpless to transform the wider world, some critics have worked to create small worlds: utopian microcosms where relationships of authority are reversed. The goal is to establish oneself at the centre of a small world, at a distance from a wider world from which nothing is now expected. These plebeian worlds, rich in ideas and initiatives, sometimes exemplary in their graceful renewal of democratic moments, can also develop as places of utter confusion where people reinvent hot water, establish new "social contracts" with all the flaws of the old ones, and carry out the violence of original foundational acts in a manner not unlike certain totalitarian regimes, albeit on a much smaller scale. Criticism is then replaced by proselytism and black-and-white thinking.

Distraught libertarians and liberals have now re-established the semblance of a left/right political spectrum, exclusively organized around the soothing concept of "freedom." In the reality of their approaches and practices, rights and principles often look like a supermarket display of elements to be picked up and brandished depending on circumstances and interests. The motto is now "my rights" or what "I want": Who cares about anything else? The world is dislocated or has vanished, and it has become difficult to think of developing not freedoms but constraints. Working together on an equal footing to design the constraints that we want to impose on ourselves as the basis of our life in society—constraints that guarantee the possibility of freedoms for an entire world—is no longer even conceivable.

We struggle, in fact, to establish other social relationships, just as we find it impossible to think of ourselves as revolutionaries in a non-romantic way. And yet, revolution—meaning to bring down, and consign to the past, the institutions and powers that seriously damage the common good—is a task of the most immediate urgency, even if it were only a matter of safeguarding any ecosystem that can still survive the blind destruction carried out by major industry and high finance, or of getting economic decision-makers to radically change how they think about the billions of impoverished people who currently experience in their bodies a psychotic degree of exclusion.

If it is too clearly announced (or sung), revolution may become just one more version of "the game" that property owners and other worthies have always known how to play to their advantage. This is powerfully expressed in Giuseppe Tomasi di Lampedusa's novel *The Leopard*, and in Visconti's cinematographic adaptation of it: a revolutionary saga becomes a story of structural change accompanied by elites who make sure that nothing changes. To think of the revolution non-romantically implies that we have no preconceived idea of what it must be. It is more important to recognize the revolution as something belonging to the realm of necessity than to identify exclusive tactics or inevitable historical movements. Ending what harms the common good: we have now reached the point where the extensive destruction of ecosystems must stop, along with extractive exploitation that grinds and crushes people, and financial dynamics that keep on deepening the excruciating gap between rich and poor. Perhaps circumstances themselves will consign to the past the institutions that harm the common good, but this too may be a tragedy if nothing is done to change the course that is currently leading us to catastrophe.

Calls to action take place in a state of now manifest confusion. What should we do? Let's do anything. Whenever an attitude frees us from the harmful ways of mediocrity, whenever an idea helps us develop a justly instituted public life, these will be ways for us to move forward, without any guarantees. According to Patrice Loraux, "left-wing politics are politics that don't know where they are going."[3] We need to leave the road leading to predictable chaos and establish a road that suburban dwellers will be willing to take when they begin to doubt; this may well happen on the day when a full tank of gas costs more than a day's pay. When the ideological chorus becomes dissonant, it will be time, with sovereign power, for us to make the break together—time for an act of co-rupture instead of corruption. This is Pascal's wager adapted to politics. We can act as if our actions necessarily tend to bring down an order that creates large-scale devastation while asserting its right to spoonfeed us; we can look forward to the day when the majority's trust in this order's discourse will falter; we can count on the garish visibility of its duplicity; we can move forward, trusting that self-criticism, and a deep caution, will be part of our way of thinking; and if we believe that our actions are destined to succeed in history, these actions can take place in reality, as the opportunity arises, and bring us to a wider space.

Co-rupture

At this stage, the issue of corruption goes beyond the influence peddling, cash-filled envelopes, and preferential treatment with which it is usually associated. These are only symptoms. Corruption is something much more serious: it is a process of radical deterioration that has a profoundly negative impact on what is essential.

An ancient work, Aristotle's *On Generation and Corruption*, helps define the concept on the basis of two aspects. In this work, he explains that corruption does not occur when something is simply altered or corroded, in the sense that some of its attributes or characteristics change. For instance, a metal rod that goes from hot to cold is certainly altered, but not yet corrupted. There is corruption only when something is so deeply transformed that its nature can no longer be recognized. It occurs "not in virtue of aggregation or segregation [of its constituent elements], but when something changes from this to that as a whole."[4] A thing becomes corrupted when it is changed in its permanent elements. When a seed becomes wheat, it is corrupted in order to generate something else. The process causes something to arise that is different in its most basic components.

Aristotle's propositions then suggest that we define corruption as a process that eventually comes to an end. Corruption plays itself out. It reaches completion. In this sense, corruption is not marginal damage, a limited evil, a superficial mark. We need to understand it as an attack. We cannot keep on defining it as a threat or a mere corrosive element: we need to think about its outcome. Thinking about the process of corruption calls for positive reflection on its results. Because corruption has consequences, dealing with it necessarily implies identifying what follows: the new thing that appears at the end of the process. We have gone from one state to another: What are these two states?

Corruption cannot be eternal. There is nothing that could be described as an endless process of "corruptance." Corruption is an action that, in working out the radical transformation that it embodies, reaches its conclusion. In terms of political mores and public life, for instance, we cannot speak of the corruption of public institutions and principles over decades without inquiring what has happened to them as a result of the deep changes to which we are giving this name.

Historically and collectively, we have now reached the point where we can say that there has been corruption. And this being the case, what have we come to? Where do we now find ourselves, and what are we facing?

This is the work of philosophy: not to be satisfied with specialized knowledge of the classics as a source of models of abstract order, in relation to which scholars can negatively assess the contingent order of things, but to create concepts through which we can grasp the new order arising from corruption as it plays itself out. How can we name, think, and organize the radically new thing, structure, or organization that ensues from corruption? We no longer say that corruption indefinitely threatens democracy, but that the principle of democracy, now corrupt, gives rise to a new regime described by the word "governance." The corrupt university ends up as an institution that is in the business of selling expertise. The corrupt economy gives rise to the financial oligarchy. Corrupt judicial institutions lead to expensive private bodies for the settlement of disputes. We cannot, of course, be content with mere slogans or labels. We must define the forms of these new institutions, understand how they work, and see how, once again, we can get in their way.

Let us therefore view the democratic principle as corrupted. One example is the way in which the managerial transformation of the world is accomplished, in people's minds, under the name of governance. Public institutions are caricatured as a den inhabited by people who cannot be trusted: a clique of privileged actors (civil servants and tenured staff). Opinion makers assert that this clique should be contained, in order to block the threat they embody, by the private sector and associations representing the interests of "civil society." Citizenship is now understood as an aggregate of people advocating for private interests in the manner of small lobbyists. The system's intention is simple: these unequal actors must now form partnerships, with the smallest players attempting to graft their small interests onto those of the big players. When a multinational decides to drill somewhere, for instance, members of the community must figure out how this action could be locally meaningful. Partnership is a moral imperative: both sides must be equally open, even though the power dynamic is so utterly unequal. Meanwhile, the strongest ideas born of the history of democracy, such as the people, the commonwealth, or the public welfare, quietly disappear.

Let us also view the idea of a state founded on law as an idea that has been profoundly transformed by tax havens and other accommodating jurisdictions. States competing with each other to attract now sovereign investors have entered into a spiral of fiscal, regulatory, and judicial dumping. Legal and tax havens are no longer to be found only among typically recognizable states such as the Bahamas, Luxembourg, or Singapore—they also include Canada, Delaware, Austria, Ireland, and Côte d'Ivoire. Countries "offshorize" entire sections of their laws in order to organize administrative laisser faire zones to the benefit of big industrial, financial, and organized crime groups that have long been operating transnationally, that is, independently of state frameworks.

Finally, let us agree that the regime in which we now find ourselves no longer threatens democracy, but has already carried out its threats. Let us call it plutocracy, oligarchy, parliamentary tyranny, financial totalitarianism, or something else. Let us debate how best to define the basis of this ultra-private power. One of its characteristics, which certainly identifies it as an oligarchy, is its ability to capture and encode any social activity so that it becomes a part of the process of capitalization enriching those who are enthroned at the top of the hierarchy. Singing, stamp collecting, hitting a ball with a bat, reading Balzac, or building motors: whatever it is, the oligarchy makes sure that any socialized activity, however slight, is inserted into a system that manages inscriptions and codes to benefit the concentration of power at the top. Every human activity is organized in such a way as to increase the capital of those who oversee aggregated operations. This makes us poor in every way.

Once we have found the right name for these regimes, we are then required to resist them, if we are democrats, or even undertake to overthrow them. This means making a break with the new order, enforcing a rupture with harmful and destructive dynamics, and collectively emancipating ourselves. It is a break that we must make together: a co-rupture.

It is our turn to fundamentally change the established regime. From now on, we are the corrupting force. We need to carry out a co-rupture with these terrible forms in order to generate new ones.

Let us return to our classical philosopher, Aristotle. For him, there was no corruption without generation. "The generation of one thing in the case of substances is always the corruption of another and the corruption of one thing the generation of another."[5] A new situation is generated on the basis of the situation that has been made obsolete. Generating and corrupting are produced by the same power. What distinguishes these two actions?

Aristotle does not provide explicit moral value judgments, but he does tend to record generation on the positive side of the ledger. What is generated is what tends toward the better, and corruption, consequently, is what tends toward the worse. Aristotle gives the example of knowledge, which belongs to generation, while ignorance belongs to corruption.[6]

Without stretching the meaning of the text, we can say that generation relates to the positive outcome of a process of radical transformation. Taking these words further, we can say that a political program that embodies the tension between corruption and generation would lead us to design a political project that aims to bring about a substantial transformation of society into forms that we believe desirable.

Here and now, we are developing a wider ability to name a complex reality: a process of corruption, causing us to mourn the best ideas that we had collectively developed; and a process that generates emancipatory red squares, Occupy movements, spring uprisings, and other renewals, which, despite their many flaws, continue their attempts to undermine and subvert the foundations of mediocratic institutions.

EPILOGUE:
THE POLITICS OF
THE EXTREME CENTRE

§1

AT A CERTAIN POINT, European communists, socialists, and social democrats began to describe themselves as *left-wing, but* . . . We're leftists, but not Stalinists! We don't want to make public institutions bureaucratic. We don't want excessive nationalization. We don't want corporate taxes to be too high: business needs "stimulation." We don't want a mandatory shorter work week. We don't want to welcome the kind of people who are easily identified as "dangerous classes" and other "foreign elements." At the time, a person's political allegiance was defined by the gap between enshrined "left-wing values" and the political programs that were supposed to embody them. However, not everyone has what it takes to be André Gide, whose criticism of the USSR in 1936 shocked Stalin's sycophants and helped redefine positions on the French left, but who never lost sight of basic progressive principles. With so many claiming to be *left-wing, but*, left-wing values were eventually emptied of their content through successive measures that contradicted them. Political programs identified as left-wing—although identical in every respect with the neoliberal or ultraliberal theses they claimed to oppose—ended up by corrupting even the definition of left-wing values. Who, in the United Kingdom, can forget Tony Blair's breathless admiration for "wealth creators," or Margaret Thatcher's remark that her greatest achievement was "Tony Blair and New Labour"? Who could have imagined, when the German social democratic left took power under Gerhard Schröder, that the only outcome would be austerity programs aimed at the poor? Who, in France, can forget hearing Laurent Fabius, a "socialist" party man if ever there was one, call on the left's "eternal" values as he recited the holy names of liberty, equality, fraternity, and "*laïcité*" (secularism), while completely omitting socialism's most basic premise: the concerted development, through the collective will, of public constraints on the intentions of the powerful? Who can forget hearing Michel Rocard, standard-bearer of a similar "second left wing," call for an "end to ideology," for the greater good of alliances with the powerful private sector? From this perspective, the only thing to be done was to provide the lower classes with tools to deal with the dynamics of competition—whether between wage-earners, businesses, or states—under the pretext of "knowing the economy" and trying to reach a "compromise" between classes, instead of working to move beyond this stage in history. Socialists have identified more closely with the word *but* than with the word *socialist*. From standstill to retreat, from retreat to withdrawal, from withdrawal to surrender, the French "left" has allowed itself to be represented, regressively, by the following: a future director of the IMF; a physician specializing in lucrative capillary implants, and former lobbyist, who became the minister responsible for the budget while using Swiss banks to defraud his own government; and a parvenu straight out of the Rothschild bank.

§2

In English-speaking North America, it's the other way around. The word "liberal" has the same roots in English and French, but on the basis of two distinct political traditions, it assigns people to different locations: on the left (in English) or on the right (in French). In the United States, people therefore describe themselves as *liberals, but on the left*. The left/right axis has shifted so much in response to the rule of the powerful that just displaying a mild degree of "liberalism," in the North American sense, can make you look like a revolutionary. At most, you will advocate for formal rights while leaving systemic structures unharmed. *Liberals, but on the left* never give priority to what a collectivity might become. The political tune they hum seems to be about monetary policy, the worship of money, the myth of individual success, submission to private organizations, consumerist frenzy, and smug patriotism; new couplets on specific new rights are added now and then. The only things that matter are interactions between individuals conforming to certain types; these interactions are defined and organized by a symbolic system inscribing "privilege" above everyone's head. Only the imperious psychology of these symbols can be the object of critique. Political and social institutions are a matter of concern in that they must let people in according to intersectional criteria of age, colour, nationality, gender and sexual orientation; belonging to one of these social categories may eventually replace former principles of legitimacy. Minorities suddenly discover that their fierce struggles and historic organized resistance will essentially have provided career liberals with the goods they desperately needed to display in their electoral windows, and that liberals will ask for their votes, but in a caricatural form. Liberals do not attack advertising as an institution; they want people who are usually marginalized to appear in ads, with dignity, selling detergent. They don't care that the university is functioning like a sausage factory, as long as faculty and graduate students are guaranteed recognition of their specific identities. *Left liberals* practise political action by example: they drive a car, but it's a small one; they drink cow's milk, but the cow was happy; they like to consume, but they choose fair trade products; they apply management theories, but friendly ones; they aggressively sell products, but noble ones; they take planes, but they have carbon credits; they vote for parties that are capitalist, but "liberal." Their motto is: *If only everyone did as I do.* In politics, when they must take a position, individual ethics is their preferred angle. Clearing away all the social mediations that suffocate the self, the individual would like to appear as someone who has triumphed over history—even though individualism is not the work of individuals, but an ideological construction made possible by an impoverished mimicry. This idea of the self, which does not arise from oneself and does not go without saying, tends to produce subjects who must try to save themselves by cultivating the narcissism of small differences. Supporting a distant orphanage or collecting Chinese teapots become the centre of a distinction that is more important than anything else. In times like these, it is in any case imperative to establish a strong self in order to abuse others, and to make up for a lack of social justice by referring to communities based on a sociological denominator that was once emancipatory: gender, colour, religion, sexual orientation, and so on. The fact that Derridean deconstruction, May '68, feminism, the gay and lesbian movement, or environmental demands were not originally intended to be liberal does not prevent them from being inexorably drawn into a liberal application. Subjects must use these interlocking criteria to weave the unique fabric of their singularity. Finally an element will arise that will ensure the ipseity (selfhood) of the person, endowing him or her with meaning: the customized pages of social media, veritable press agencies of the self, peddling the good news.

§3

Historically, in North America, the left/right political spectrum has essentially been based on ways of qualifying liberalism. From left to right, people can be identified as left libertarian, North American style liberal, European style liberal, neoliberal, ultraliberal, right libertarian. The first see freedom as an opportunity to emancipate ourselves from the problems inherited from Western-centred, patriarchal, bourgeois history. The second agree, but, lacking imagination, they believe that ideological structures can never be bypassed. The third babble on about the virtues of freedom, with a concern for pure concepts that often leads them to overlook the practical issues of the day; for them, words like "justice" and "communication" are powerful mantras. As for neo- and ultraliberals, they are willing to admit, to varying degrees, that freedom inevitably contributes to the development of forms of systemic domination; this is seen as a necessity. They are fond of metaphors taken from nature, and vulgar Darwinism is a key reference. Finally, right libertarians claim to be openly at war against all social structures, except big business, which is seen as a paragon. There is something for every taste in this display of choices regarding freedom—which perfectly illustrates the system that provides the display.

§4

The toughest tend toward an unambiguous and openly proclaimed anarchism. They are often driven to this position by the brutality of capitalism. Few in number, they are almost alone in embodying the power of the negative and are doing useful work in this respect. When they practise dumpster diving, they crudely reveal the grotesque reality of agro-industrial productivism. When they mock political parties and non-governmental organizations, they are in fact denouncing the infantile nature of electoral and civic campaigns. When they refuse to vote, they shed light on the deeply tendentious quality of electoral processes. When they boycott labour unions, they emphasize the unions' spinelessness. When they plunder chic boutiques or department stores, they foreground class relations in processes of production, distribution, and urban development. When they challenge police forces, they show these forces' brutal power. When feminists in this movement declare war on alpha males, they also challenge the ordinary domination the patriarchy grants to lawmakers, scientists, bosses, and husbands. So many authorities and rulings are illegitimate! In doing this work, the anarchists sometimes reach the point where they are also "negative" in a more prosaic sense: disenchanted, on edge, they may eventually lose their vitality. "Fuck everything!" was long the rallying cry for groups of this tendency in Quebec—groups that have much in common with small French organizations involved in perpetually rearranging the molecules of the revolution that is to come. From their point of view, as far as representative democracy is concerned, the case is dismissed: democracy should always be carried out directly in the here and now, and modern political institutions have dug its grave. If activists of this kind ever read Saskia Sassen, presumably they only feel contempt. In *Territory, Authority, Rights*, she notes that while legislative and judicial powers have undoubtedly accompanied capital as it subjugated peasants, women, workers, and colonized peoples, they have also been the vector through which these groups have attempted to reverse historical relationships to obtain rights and guarantees.[1] Because such attempts have led to entirely unsatisfactory outcomes, the anarchists proclaim the independence of their own political clan on a self-sufficient plebeian basis. Making a break becomes a key idea, especially in the context of a system embodying white civilization, money, and the more powerful gender, among other things. What does it matter if fighting against elections actually gives elections more importance than the average voter is inclined to assign them? What matters is to demonstrate the fact of opposition and to show how inventive one can be. Against the army, against the media, against the patriarchal order, against bourgeois culture, against ossified jurisdictions, against the university, against any educational curriculum, against political parties, against the representative system, against capitalism, and against business, they favour, to the contrary, their own communion made visible by tangible action. Converging on their own private lair, they celebrate, as a group, their victory over the illusions still cultivated by the fools that surround them. Here they recover their true subjectivity; now it is their turn to believe in freedom. Within these communities, there are moments of grace that may be delineated in novels—necessarily rough-grained—such as *Brief Summer of Anarchy* by Hans Magnus Enzensberger:

> A great wave of emotion swept over the crowd.
>
> For some reason, or by mistake, two bands were invited to play at the ceremony; one played at a very low volume, the other very loudly. . . . It was not possible to organize the free passage of a funeral cortege through this chaos. . . . You could hear the tones, but the melody was unrecognizable. Everyone's fists were still raised in the air. The music finally stopped, the fists descended and then you could hear the noise of the crowd amidst which Durruti reposed on the shoulders of his comrades. . . .
>
> No, these were not the funeral rites of a king; this was a burial ceremony organized by the people.[2]

Such impulses of solidarity are not exempt, however, from the authoritarian or even fascistic tendencies that are latent in every political situation. Charismatic power cannot fail to emerge, as it does wherever humans organize. As in other social settings, drugs are sometimes the bitter remedy employed to cope with deep trauma inflicted by the hated regime. And when things get out of hand, undesirables betrayed by their actions or by slander are pushed back to unofficial margins by improvised courts. Replaying day one of the social contract, the group often finds a new Leviathan emerging somewhere nearby. A propensity to challenge contemporary institutions of power cannot be taken for victory over the insistent question of the social bond, always present here and everywhere else.

§5

Our lack of collective thought is so acute that we were recently glad to see it appear in the blurry numerical contours of the "99 per cent." The Occupy movement defined itself through opposition to a ruling class that rejoices in belonging to the "1 per cent." Occupy was a fragile synthesis of radical movements and *liberal-but* leftists. It was rife with internal tensions, and its fragile unity was based less on an idea than on a feeling: "indignation."* Traditional emancipatory movements are themselves the setting for consummate forms of discrimination, which intersectional approaches bring to the fore except when they are fostering ever finer microdistinctions leading to microdefinition of a marginal self. Our thinking about what we hold in common and have been given to share is no longer seen as an opportunity to include, in the greater collective whole, social groups that have been marginalized or viewed as minorities; instead, such centripetal thinking is seen as a way of confining them to an alienating and oppressive common realm, which is dishonestly presented as immobilized in a hegemonic stance that has contributed to these groups' suffering. Proliferating centrifugal identities, and the conquest of meaning at the margins, are now viewed as redemptive.

Of course, political minorities often approach the issues of their time in a way that goes beyond exclusively sectarian or identitarian concerns. To deny this would be a sign of ignorance or bad faith: the women's move-

---

* A reference to a bestselling pamphlet by French author Stéphane Hessel, *Indignez-vous!* (2010), published in English as *Time for Outrage*. The Spanish translation, *¡Indignaos!*, provided the name for *Los Indignados*, a widespread movement against austerity and corruption that emerged in Spain in 2011.—*CB*

ment addresses issues related to social justice in the widest sense, just as the Indigenous rights movement addresses environmental issues, and these are but two examples among many. And yet, we have to acknowledge that these associations have not given rise to any powerful concept conducive to shaping institutions that would energize the community as a whole, beyond each movement's specific base, nor to images that would convey this wider community's pride. A propensity to dissociate oneself from everyone else takes precedence over reasons to come together. At certain times, public figures—Lula, Morales, Correa, Mélenchon, Tsipras, Corbyn, Aung San Suu Kyi, Iglesias Turrión, Sanders—step forward to embody the motley aspirations of a crowd that is always on the verge of breaking up: institutional structures relentlessly push these figures to the margin or mechanically bring them to the centre, unless they are simply snubbed by their chosen supporters. No form of coalition has been able to prevent its forces from crumbling in this way. Ultimately, to *speak as* (a Black woman, a worker, a wage earner, a peasant, a person living with HIV, and so on) will certainly lead to emancipation from the generality of patriarchal criteria, but going beyond mere political recognition, this emancipation will benefit forces stimulating the development of singular characteristics. *Liberal-but* leftists resistant to the totems of high civilization distribute any overall political claims among a range of singular, not to say quirky, causes. They act like the low centre of gravity of a regressive spiral.

§6

An unexpected political figure appears in this landscape: one who is *right-wing, but* . . . Having lost any kind of swagger, these people are aware of the disastrous consequences of the hegemonic regime that they defended for so long, and now aspire to rein in. Things have gone too far, there is a lack of control, irrationality prevails. They do not condemn the system itself, but the excesses of those who, thanks to it, have not been regulated in any way. No one asks if these excesses might not be specifically related to the regime's mafia-like premises. There are any number of such critics. The most famous, Joseph Stiglitz, formerly initiated in the mysteries of the World Bank, now denounces the imbecility of capitalism. He blames powerful states for having let big money force poor countries to enact economic measures that they would never have adopted for themselves. Marc Roche, *Le Monde*'s financial correspondent in London, says he is now "a doubting liberal" after having followed the vagaries of Goldman Sachs, a bank that stands for conflict of interest throughout the world thanks to the many former partners it has put in key positions in state apparatuses and the many former political leaders it has recruited. Roche is alarmed to see tax havens authorizing illegal practices that would be severely penalized in any state, however placid, that was governed by the rule of law. Multibillionaire Warren Buffett is dismayed to learn that his secretary pays taxes at a higher rate than he does. Larry Fink, *primus inter pares* among the great shareholder rentiers, berates his fellows whose greed for dividends causes them to dismember the big companies that produce them. George Soros wonders why the contemporary financial system allows him to speculate merrily on the world's various currencies, giving him the power, simply as a wealthy individual, to bring about the collapse of an entire national economy. The Rockefellers have withdrawn from all oil projects for environmental reasons. François Dupuy, who teaches in business schools, denounces the intellectual laziness of pseudo-management theorists and their fetishistic use of ideas. Christine Lagarde, IMF managing director and member of the upper bourgeoisie, scolds Western governments for enacting violent and sterile austerity budgets, year after year, to the detriment of their populations. All claim to be *right-wing, but* . . . A minimum of political awareness and intellectual honesty leads them to see the formidable failure of a political system whose growth principle means that by definition, it has no limit.

§7

Studying the genesis of bourgeois parliamentarianism in France from 1795 to 1820, historian Pierre Serna presents the "extreme centre" as revolving around recantations. His Republic of Turncoats is made up of politicians who are calm, levelheaded, and sound managers of public affairs, but who maintain their position by ceaselessly going back on their word, repeatedly enacting "the unscrupulous about-faces made possible by vicissitudes." Gradually there is a shift from a period where being faithful to one's convictions may lead to death to another, corrupt period in which "as soon as it is given, one's word, fragile, ephemeral, changing, is damaged, eroded, limited, worn-out, hollowed out by the passing of time, by the very conditions of existence as it continues on its way, relentlessly, outside of the ideality traced in the suspended time of the promise."³ But to think of today's extreme centre in these terms would be to pay it too great a tribute. Since the Third Republic, often dominated by liberal (known at the time as radical) parties who had mastered the art of blowing hot and cold to an exasperating degree, and which was followed by an era of political semanticists and communicators cultivating equivocation at the very origin of thought, the technocrats of politics have learned to do without (economize on) the moment of conviction. You're not going back on your word if you never said anything. A lexical compendium found at the French École nationale d'administration teaches students to speak in what the French call *langue de bois*, wooden language, the language of stereotypical platitudes. As financial globalization deprives them of any real power, they spend their university days practising the rhetoric of a pointless ethos.

§8

In presenting himself as "normal" and making this normality the ersatz basis of his program, the Socialist Party candidate who won the presidential election in France in 2012 was chiefly successful in decreeing that every-thing not normal was pathological. His was a quasi-formal restoration of an extreme centre in which extremism took the form of intolerance toward anything that did not coincide with an arbitrarily proclaimed juste milieu. Anything that established power presented as normal—with all the threat-ening connotations of a word that seems unchallengeable—was seen as such, including the racism of the state, police brutality, increasingly pre-carious work, the unlimited sovereignty assigned to banks, the autonomy multinationals achieve through their subsidiaries, the trivialization of poli-tics, dependence on oil and nuclear energy, and the forced cohabitation of opposites disguised as a "synthesis." These wrongs placidly achieved the status of norms. The average, under this system, in no way derives from an analysis of possibilities that is summarized by an abstraction: it imposes itself in action and dictates what standards must be observed. If Honoré Daumier had produced a bust of an elected representative to include among his Celebrities of the Juste Milieu, he would have called it *The Mediocre One*, giving it the puffy features of a man who has no expres-sion because he is attempting to show all of them. François Hollande, however, believed he was draping himself in dignity as he gratuitously orchestrated this situation: "Compromise is not a subtle balance, an in-between, a mediocre average point. Compromise is the opposite of this: it is a commitment."[4] There are also very high doses of "communica-tions." Within the nominal left, it has become impossible to insist on the critique of social democracy by pointing out that it helps to perpetuate capitalism, driving the system's destructive power to its ultimate limit. And yet, is there anyone who still doesn't know that our ecosystems' abil-ity to handle productivist growth rates is now coming to an end? Does anyone not understand that liberal initiatives help widen the gap between rich and poor? Instead of these analyses, preference is given to hackneyed generalizations—any port in a storm, every cloud has a silver lining—and exhortations to pragmatism. All of this causes our mental apparatus to rigidify, and a series of labels, always available to annihilate criticism—

the "far left," "terrorism," "populism," "archaism," "extremism"—prevent thought from renewing itself.

§9

Is it because proletarians do not become involved in public life that the media and political parties do not talk about them, or is it the other way around? On November 4, 2014, a headline on Radio-Canada's website asked: "Do you belong to the middle class?" Readers were invited to take a quiz to learn the answer. According to Université de Sherbrooke researchers quoted on the site, one-half of all Canadians belong to this vast social category. What about the others? Not a word. They are simply outside the frame: neither rich nor poor, neither bourgeois nor proletarian, neither colonizer nor colonized. The magazine *Les Affaires* does an even better job: "Which middle class do you belong to?" is the question it asked on October 21, 2015. A diversity of existences are possible, but only within the "middle class." If you are a middle-class person in North America who reads a mainstream newspaper or listens to a respected broadcaster every day, you still won't know anything about the daily existence of someone living on welfare in your country. In Quebec, for instance, how do people manage to live on an income of $623 a month, while facing generalized contempt? You will also be ignorant of the world of labour. If you happen to get up early one day, you will rediscover the existence of people—many of whom are immigrants—whose working day began long before you usually leave for the office. Nor will you know anything about the decadent way of life of the ruling class, the one that appropriates the wealth produced by the people it hires—while pretending to create it—in order to satisfy its craving for pomp and power. Nor will you suspect that they or their ancestors often used criminal methods to amass their fortune. Meanwhile, you will have thousands of opportunities to hear journalists or columnists discuss the gadgets that you might acquire, the money you might borrow, conventional jobs that will be created or lost, and the vacation packages that everyone seems to love. The media invite you to leave everything else on the garbage heap of a world without history.

§10

This is what it's about: getting people in the middle class to forget that they will never be anything but proletarians with money, and that they have no control over the economic and social parameters that shape their standard of living. Inexorably, so many things elude them: the urban planning model in which they live, the price of oil and raw materials that determine their lives, the interest rates and currency markets that keep them in debt, consumption habits and professional advantages (clothes, telephones, cars provided by their employer) that serve to distract them. The "clients" that they are forced to become do not really choose all of these flavours of the month—it's more like having them rammed down their throat. The world they occupy is only theirs on loan. The "middle class" is like the hotel doorman in F.W. Murnau's film *Der letzte Mann* who leaves his poor neighbourhood every morning and comes back every evening, admired by his fellows because of his fine clothes: since he works in the hotels of the bourgeoisie, he is always dressed to the nines. But the uniform he wears has been assigned to him for work—it does not belong to him. One day, his boss demotes him and takes away his uniform. He turns away, ashamed, for the first time dressed in the rags that genuinely reflect his social status. That day, he is jolted into understanding that clothes do not make the man, but this insight does not seem powerful enough for him to apply it to members of other social categories and say that the king, too, has no clothes. He resembles people who vote for parties of the extreme centre because they want to maintain intact the mirages of private property, as part of their belief in those for whom the system is actually meaningful.

§11

Despite the system's failures, liberalism is so hegemonic that even those who challenge it compose in its key to make sure their little music is heard. The political allegiance of Quebec historian Éric Bédard, walking in the steps of the New Philosophers, constitutes one example. Bédard says that he is a "conservative" because he wants to challenge activists inspired by May '68 and the limitless self-actualization that they stand for. But no sooner has he claimed this designation than he tries to distinguish himself from those with whom he shares it: right-libertarians who have made the individual subject into something holy, ultraliberals obsessed with the right to accumulate capital, or religious fanatics who use divine references as a yardstick to determine the meaning of political practices. All of these currents may also be labelled "conservative." Our fine friend says that he is a "social democrat": he's a *conservative, but* . . . For him, it is sufficient to advocate for "states that attempt to articulate common rules in the name of higher principles." At this point, as he makes a distinction between his theoretical position and other conservative schools, he behaves, in fact, like a liberal. "My conservatism is first and foremost a critical attitude toward all of these progressive movements that claim to have found the meaning of History."[5] *My* conservatism—as if conservatism, an ideology that claims to embody moral values and traditions shared by all, could be shaped by someone's chosen individual preferences, when in fact such preferences are necessarily construed in relation to collective references. This is not the only flaw in Bédard's thinking: he also fails to distinguish, among the movements he challenges, those that created the social democratic state and stand for the common values that he claims to espouse, but that he wants to confine to a definitive essence and form. He omits the fact that this invigorating, shifting, and uncompromising past has never been located anywhere but in the changing vitality of radical transformations. "Conservatives" of his kind sublimate one hardly knows what immutable truth, taking a snapshot of a historical period as if the suspended moment they have identified were an acquired right to be preserved at all costs. They freeze the movements of the past, arbitrarily and abusively determining their true shapes. And yet, we are still waiting for the repercussions of these past movements to extend beyond us into the future. The French Revolution went astray and has not yet done its work: the Republic is a concept that has not yet been fully worked out. Equality between citizens has not been made reality, nor the principle that citizens, collectively, should be able to appropriately assert their will through public institutions. The American Revolution is equally unfinished. Public authority, seen as irredeemably other, can only be rejected in a self-paranoid style that precludes the development of a new constitution rooted in the here and now. These outbursts of history leave us with rights left to conquer and forms of organization yet to develop. And the best way to kill an idea will always be to try to "preserve" it.

§12

French philosopher and law historian Pierre Legendre argues that ancient religious rituals are revelations retrieved from a deep well containing the meaning of all things. However, he is the first to acknowledge that these ancient rituals are perverted by contemporary management, which uses a religious vocabulary to frame consumer choices that are actually defined by the strategies of marketing science. Forced to acknowledge the failure of the scientific management of the postwar years, organizational theorists have sought inspiration from the discourses and principles found in places of worship and major religious texts. Although war has been declared on terrorists exclusively identified as religious zealots, born-again Christians, "radicalization in God's name," "Allah's madmen," and their ilk, religious references are simultaneously retrieved by capital. Lloyd Blankfein, chief executive of Goldman Sachs, stated in 2009 that banks are "doing God's work."[6] Start-ups, surrounded by coaches, mentors, gurus, and other apostles of management, are protected by angel investors who help them take their brand to the preacher's tent. One of the great specialists in this area, Jesper Kunde, has written a reference work entitled *Corporate Religion* that tells business leaders and human resource managers how to transform their company into a sect. The aim is no less than "to unite everything in a Corporate Religion."[7] The *Financial Times* agreed to co-publish this voluminous handbook with Prentice Hall. To satisfy his thirst for metaphors, our expert in theological management reduces corporate religion to three aspects. Its first goal is to develop around the corporation and its holy brand a phantasmagorical passion detaching them from any social, historical, or political reality. A cult surrounds the corporation and its brand. Next, since religion, as its etymology indicates, is supposed to create bonds, the entrepreneurial religion will use actual forms of communion to unite its flock of believers—a flock that includes not only employees but also suppliers and consumers. These events take the form of occasional gatherings, public salons, or ceremonies. Bikers devoted to a given brand for their official rallies are a perfect example. Finally, religion is a formidable tool for manipulation. A closed community created around a logo can be manipulated through belief. This corporate theology is represented by an upward-moving graphic in which merchandise, initially ranked as a simple "product," becomes an agent of redemption as part of the "brand religion." Following this approach, a product is no longer known simply as what it is (a candy bar, a sweater, a video game console): it must be identified by its "corporate concept." Once labelled, the product provides a feeling, or, as it is known in the jargon, "added emotional value." It is no longer tissue paper, a watch, a box of dehydrated soup: these things, now that they are associated with the Kleenex, Rolex, or Lipton brands, radiate a reassuring familiarity, a sense of trust or motherly love. It doesn't stop there. The spiritual bond must extend throughout the corporation. Consumers, who are now believers, must feel attachment not only to the product, but to the corporation that provides it. An act of acknowledgement must follow: at the level of advertising, this is embodied in a highly sincere "Thank you [brand name]!" The product becomes an important element of "brand culture" when it is consubstantially a part of the cultural landscape as a kind of intrinsic heritage. Finally, it becomes a brand religion. We have now reached the final stage, nirvana: thanks to the brand, consumers/believers know that they exist, and the "corporate religion," as an entity, now attains—and this is not a joke—"brand heaven." The brand, and the company that makes it available, are now literally an object of devotion: "To the consumer they are a must, a belief." All of these borrowed expressions are bound to make us uneasy. Get stupid! is what we are told on every page. Spreading the Good News makes people so crazy that this approach, as Marie-Claude Élie-Morin points out in her book on "the dictatorship of happiness,"[8] forces employees to adopt the practices of a sect. They take positive thinking courses and are required to be cheerful and to believe in the company's activity, even when presented with sophisms that are an insult to their intelligence. In this brave new world, a company committed to such practices—Lululemon—once saw an employee lose her head and murder a coworker.[9]

§13

The left/right spectrum now takes so many forms that it too seems to be offered as part of the market abundance that the liberal regime glorifies. It is able to clearly summarize the dialectical tension between pacifism and militarism, the regulation of industrial activity and laissez-faire, taxing or exempting wealth, nationalizing or privatizing economic structures, a secular state or the incorporation of the divine into institutional life, the development of labour law or free negotiations between employers and workers, regional decentralization of public institutions or their concentration in the capital, attributing elective positions to members of several different social classes or monopolization of such positions by a specifically identified elite, recognizing various minorities or emphasizing traditional representations of them, attributing political decisions to bodies arising from civil society or strictly confining all discussions to the great institutions of power, a prejudice in favour of industry or environmentalism, welcoming immigrants or closing borders, believing in free trade or advocating protectionism, and so on. The list is endless, and it can give rise to endless combinations. There are so many reasons for leaders of the extreme centre to say they belong to "the left" or "the right" that ordinary people lose sight of any basic distinction or value system that could structure reality on the basis of consistent principles.

§14

As postmodernists, we find it difficult to assert that referential criteria apply to left and right. Let's follow Gérard Filoche, who in 2014 was a radical member of the Socialist Party's national executive in France, and who was pugnacious enough to stand in opposition to the government formed by his own party. The French prime minister, Manuel Valls, although he was a "socialist," chose, under the authority of the president of the Republic, to carry out a policy identical with employers' demands. Was he therefore a right-wing political actor? Innocent of any conceptual effort, Filoche replied that Valls had kept his left-wing "label"— political affiliation being strictly a matter of what one declares. Anyone can be left-wing if they want to be. In response to fears of a fratricidal era of reciprocal excommunications within the extended family of the conventional so-called left, a new left/right spectrum was created, leading Filoche to say that Valls is "on the left's extreme right," "on the edge," and probably more to the right than the most left-wing member of the nominal family of "the right." Filoche explained all this in a debate organized by the France 24 broadcasting corporation on August 27, 2014: in this debate, he declared his opposition to his own Socialist government's bill establishing a wide-ranging program in support of employers, while a business leader defended it. And we wonder why citizens are confused.

§15

The far right presents itself as a kind of mental prosthesis for voters who are weary of these intricacies. It is inhabited by the death drive, yearns for the end of complex thought, and believes that the removal of all difference will solve everything. Its goal is less to help build a people (of whatever kind) than to demand that the people be confined to a rigid representation held up to it like a mirror. The people is required to believe that this misshapen and simplistic image reveals its essence as a people, and that anything contradicting the image is a form of adversity that must be expelled from the public landscape. Depending on the era, the fantasy prevails that once the Jew, the Arab, the Black person, the gay person, the Muslim—or some other figure, such as the corrupt elite, that does not coincide with the idea of the unified subject—is assimilated or expelled, the people, at last reduced to itself in conceptual terms, will experience in a deep sleep the comfort of being at one with itself.

§16

Although the extreme centre seeks to suppress the antagonism between left and right, and is fairly successful in doing so with appeals to rationality, level-headedness, pragmatism, and realism, it also creates adversarial reactions whose creed is "telling it like it is." These adversaries, glorifying everything that is not "politically correct," will view any kind of foul language as proof of authenticity. Media that we are unwilling to describe by their true name as fascist are called "trash radio" or "alt-right" in North America, while the same pathological verbosity is found in Europe, especially in the virulent debates carried out on social media. A policy of crude, outrageous, and excessive speech takes the place of healthy oppositional discourse, to the point where candidates to their country's highest elected positions reproduce this speech with astonishing self-assurance. Few of the people who are seduced by this reptilian approach will remember the actual content of the speakers' vociferations, whether on platforms that are far too big for them or in tiny webcam settings. As long as their "straight talk," "plain common sense," and "telling it like it is" are associated with the aesthetic posture of supposedly saying out loud what the majority silently thinks, there will be supporters who claim victory over established elites with their political correctness and institutional conformism. Slogans are felt to be sufficient. Faced with this hegemonic mindset, mental surrender seems to be the only option, with intellectual hastiness leading to violence that will take care of the rest. The chief strength of these champions is that they never face an opponent. Anyone who engages with them will be corrupted to the point of resembling them.

§17

As an implicit theme, violence is an issue. It encloses the public debate between traditionalists, who are elated when the state uses violence in the name of a cruel reality principle calling for "tough choices," and advocates of the extreme centre, who also enjoy violence while appearing to be resigned to it. It is hardly surprising, then, that the sluggish currents of the extreme centre should regularly be disturbed by opportunists thrilled by evocations of the violent sources of Western power. Alternating between the roles of troublemaker and herald of unvarnished truth, these frightening actors from the margin have no inhibition in bringing up the dark origins of a state that the extreme centre wants to present as reassuring. Did not power establish itself through war, conquest, humiliation, and submission, or even deportation and extermination? Should we not return to this source to provide the state with strength and authority, or perhaps increase its virility, which is always seen as insufficiently asserted or lost? Setting up this dialectic is a godsend for the extreme centre. Thanks to the agitators, it can hope to carry out exactly the same policies while laying claim to what it really cares about and the source of its motivation: respectability.

§18

A left-wing politics worthy of the name will not consist of speaking a language that timidly supplies the debate with a few new inflections. It will provide a way of thinking about social organization that is based on a grammar embodying proletarians' distinctive grip on the course of history. The left, if it is truly a left, will necessarily work to develop mediations that give substance to the will of collective subjects, even though we may be required to continuously revisit debates around this image. Authors as different as Jacques Rancière and Pierre Rosanvallon have shown, each in their way, that the people cannot be grasped once and for all by an authority with the definitive power to embody it, but that the people provides itself with self-awareness through aesthetic forms or sociological considerations that will always have to be debated. Hence, politics. On the left, the principles on which these dynamics are based attempt to define how the collective subject can express its will through social institutions created in its own image. These institutions, arising out of the deep professionalization of politics, define in practical terms how connections are made between problems and solutions, between drives and objects of desire. On the left, work and activity are thought of in terms of collective aspirations, suffering, and needs. On the right, the focus on work and activity is also used to create representations based on shared interests, but structurally, these representations actually favour rulers and property owners. For instance, it is said to be in the common interest to provide training for the lower classes so that they can get the jobs provided by capital holders, who know how to "create" jobs. This is misappropriation. The "nation" is also often used to conceal abusive sociological standards and military expeditions exclusively designed to advance the interests of oligarchs. Under various pretexts (making national businesses competitive, defending your race, doing your fair share), the predetermined positions of a powerful minority take precedence over those of the majority. If emancipatory movements are to arise, they will inevitably be based on class dynamics. If a government were to enact rules and standards to attenuate unbalanced power relations, we might view it as a moderate right-wing government, but not yet a left-wing one. The left seeks to emancipate itself from forms that are both selfish and perverse as it works to define a framework in which the collective subject can exchange with itself in a sovereign manner. This is how we, the people, will be able to define the constraints that we choose to give ourselves in order to administer our diversity—it being understood that our freedom will be strictly determined by these constraints. This project is unheard of, in the most literal sense, since at the moment it is not promoted anywhere.

§19

Alone and exposed to greyish, then vulgar, discourses that have finally blurred all historical reference points, the citizen, brought down to the status of mere individual, is sometimes reduced to asking where power comes from. Who decides? Sovereign authority—meaning, eventually, an antagonistic force—is hard to make out in such a landscape. When we go looking for power, we do not discover any clear opponent, but we come up against the corporate bodies, or "legal persons" (in French, "moral persons") of finance and the strawmen of industry, acting under the worldwide pressure exerted by a nebulous market and impetuous shareholders. Corporations obey the law, laws are produced by lobbyists,

lobbyists act on the media, the media pay attention to markets and how they evolve, markets are subject to the current situation, the current situation is affected by the actions of central banks, central banks are independent of governments, governments are directed by parties close to organized crime, organized crime launders its money in off-shore structures, offshore structures have become part of multinationals, multinationals are endorsed by rating agencies, rating agencies give their opinion on government budgets, government budgets are based on realism and pragmatism. Spreading like rhizomes, powers that are always partial but abusive feed the development of an intellectual genre commonly known as the conspiracy theory. This expression itself is a symptom of the deep emptiness into which contemporary public speech has fallen. The word "conspiracy" is a source of cognitive dissonance. This is a concept used in law, either to protect recognition of a genocide against those who would negate it, or, in a completely different area, as a tool for judges to define the penalties that will apply to the criminals of high finance. When it is more freely used, the word is one of the anathemas favoured by anyone who wants to stifle a discussion. "Conspiracy" is also used to describe a worrisome number of fantastic tales cultivated by a thousand and one small media. Debates surrounding the causes of the 9/11 attacks in the United States are an excellent illustration of the dead end thus reached. Official statements describe a plot hatched by a formless terrorist association, spreading from Saudi Arabia through Iraq and Afghanistan to Pakistan; opponents of this version can easily take it apart by challenging the likelihood of its images and narrative on the basis of elementary physics. That there was a plot is the only thing on which we might agree. Thought remains suspended as to how the world is actually managed. "Conspiracy theorists"—frightened by the scale of what we do not know, hurrying to fill the gaps, eager to provide the narrative with spatio-temporal depth, passionately desirous to identify guilty parties and restore truth—are interesting not so much in themselves, but as a symptom of a world that has completely lost its bearings.

§20

Themes of the extreme centre political debate are related to the phenomena of displacement and condensation that Freud analyzed as elements of the psychic work carried out in dreams. In both cases, the world is mentally reorganized around displaced symbols that one overloads with meaning instead of grappling with serious underlying issues. The carbon exchange is extensively covered, rather than ongoing environmental tragedies caused by industrial exploitation; fleeing Syrian war exiles, rather than the pipeline at the root of the conflict; how the Greek debt will be paid off, rather than the criminal arrangements that made the population responsible for this debt; parliamentary squabbles, rather than the power of multinationals; a highly profitable fight against certain forms of cancer, rather than simple dietary changes that might prevent the disease; managing the local hockey team, rather than managing the state's sovereign wealth fund. And so on. Public debate addresses the clothing that too many or too few women are or are not wearing—women, whether Muslims or Femen activists, of whom we know nothing and are not expected to—or focuses on the presumed barbarity of people identified by the colour of their skin or their origin. Out of their depth, many hold forth in a manner bordering on delirium on topics that serve to conceal crucial issues: glaciers are melting, the desert is advancing, soils are eroding, radiation is seeping from nuclear waste, global temperatures are rising, ecosystems are falling apart, the social state is collapsing, the economy now reduced to finance is utterly alienated, there is no power to counteract financial power, the conquest of resources and markets requires war, philosophical reference points are lost, and all of this in an order where individuals let themselves be managed from one week to the next by mediocre people who know how to find favour with the powerful. As Freud points out, the visible elements of a bad dream like this one cannot be construed to mean anything specific, but they do convey, in disguised form, the affects associated with issues that we are not able to bring into our awareness. A quick look at any mass-circulation newspaper is enough to confirm this. Tabloids satisfy the desires that lead us to read a newspaper—our desire to learn, to be moved, to express ourselves, to analyze, to criticize, to acknowledge—but these desires are deflected. Our learning takes place in the first pages, which stridently describe phenomena that seem both freakish and uncontrollable. We are moved by the personal advice column, or the arts page; we express ourselves through columnists' brief invectives; we analyze, but only the extensive data on the sports page; and we are comforted at last for the world's turbulence by the sweetness of advertising. The newspaper continues to offer what we expect, but it fragments our subjective responses by directing them toward objects that have no relationship to each other or to whatever originally caused our response. The newspaper creates tension through its stress-inducing sections, and then soothes it through its coverage of frivolous issues. The medium attempts not to help readers think about historical vicissitudes but to plunge us into a world of darkness and fury that it alone will be able to help us endure.

§21

We can understand that no Nietzschean figure is coming forward today to denounce the "mediocrity" of "small people" who try to take a position "in the middle," at equal distance from everything.[10] The disdain cultivated people once felt for fearful beings who favoured compromise and moderation is a thing of the past. Modernity is no longer there. The word mediocrity can no longer be used in this sense. Or if it is used in this sense, legitimist sociologists such as Luc Boltanski will quickly identify the haughty speaker as a "man of *ressentiment*"[11]—an intellectual superfluous to the needs of teaching institutions, a potential conspiracy theorist, himself a mediocre being who has turned his self-hatred against society as a whole. Today, we do not criticize people who hobble their way through life for their lack of pugnacity and vitality: we know they are acting under orders. Established powers do not deplore average behaviour, they make it obligatory. A new kind of mediocracy is being instituted. Mediocrity is no longer associated, as members of the elite imagined in the nineteenth century, with self-taught intellectuals and shop owners, convinced of their own inferiority, who laboriously try to acquire the knowledge and partake of the arts reserved for the elite. Mediocracy is now embodied in professional standards, research protocols, auditing processes, and methodological calibrations that dominant organizations develop to make their subordinates interchangeable. This is the order in which craftwork gives way to function, practices to techniques, skill to implementation. The history of this order has been written by Michel Foucault (who analyzed how the army shaped "the air of the soldier"),[12] Karl Marx, Frederick Taylor (on extreme forms of industrial division of labour), Hannah Arendt (on blindly carrying out administrative commands), Georg Simmel, and C. Wright Mills (on the unthinking performances of subsidized scholars). When work became a means of subsistence for the poor and a means of producing market value for the rich, it was obvious that it, too, would require an average format.

§22

The university makes clear that it has been led astray whenever it bases its authority on something other than the mind's ability to produce meaning. This is the case, for instance, when it makes professors into brokers selling research findings to funders. However, scholars may sometimes transcend themselves, even when they lack all critical distance, when perverse undertakings are the object of their study. Mats Alvesson and André Spicer, from the business schools of Lund University and the City University of London, are completely serious as they analyze how "functional stupidity" prevails over reason in organizations dominated by greed; they even provide learned arguments in favour of such stupidity. "Functional stupidity refers to an absence of reflexivity, a refusal to use intellectual capacities in other than myopic ways, and avoidance of justifications."[13] The banality of evil has become science, for curiosity in the workplace must be castrated. We must not try to understand, but instead confine our thinking to the institution's well-worn paths in order to make sure we are functioning according to its requirements. This helps us grasp why so many representatives of authority know that they are stupid, and why a subordinate who does something heinous like quoting *Mediocracy* at work may be summoned before a disciplinary committee for a humiliating reprimand. It's not exactly that authorities don't want the truth to be spoken: no one is sincerely committed to taking the organization's lexicon seriously. However, it is very important to smother the sovereign laughter that this lexicon provokes, so that the spectacle of its vanity is never shattered. A "standardization consultant" must not be made to feel like a mere accountant. Semantic emptiness is obligatory for managers who must count on employees to do anything they are asked. This is why, during a job interview, a boss may ask candidates whether they are able to "tolerate ambiguity." In the managerial vocabulary documented by Alvesson and Spicer, there is literally a need to know if people are "foolish," that is, whether they are able to confine thought to the stage that comes before thinking, in order never to reach the stage of thought itself. We are reminded of the attitude that enabled sleepwalking brokers, throughout the first decade of this century, to keep on buying preposterous stock market products bearing dishonest triple A ratings, thus eventually plunging the planet into one of history's worst financial crises. According to Alvesson and Spicer:

> March (1996) argues that "foolishness" is required in complex environments with ambiguous goal preferences. Foolishness is an exploratory kind of reasoning whereby we act before we think. "Foolish" action helps to clarify, shape, and test preferences. It allows trial through action and imperviousness to feedback. This facilitates new

activities which have yet to show evidence of being successful (March, 2006). Here, the high level of ambiguity simply prevents people from mobilizing their cognitive capacities fully, and acting rationally.[14]

§23

A typology of five conceptual figures emerges to embody possible reactions to the hegemony of the system that demands mediocrity. Novelist Pierre Lefebvre's "broken" or "dead broke" man (the French can mean both)[15] and Georges Perec's "man asleep"[16] both refuse the established order by withdrawing from it. They hunker down beneath the times. Under the radar, these spongers or ascetics unhesitatingly choose precariousness, refusing the drollery or freakishness of the contemporary organization. As Lefebvre explains, "The true and single reason why I was not able to keep most of my jobs is pretty simple: I was never able to get used to my status as a 'human resource.'"[17] They are not primarily motivated by a desire for political resistance; they act the way they do because of an instinctive disgust and in order to preserve themselves. The second figure is the one who is mediocre by default. This unfortunate person believes the lies he is told, for since childhood, he has been entitled to nothing else. He is a good guy, ideologues like him, and he subscribes to their theories because they have become part of the structure of his subjectivity. Everything that results from the practices of our times strikes him as utterly natural. True, he suffers; he may take sleeping pills at night and guzzle coffee in the morning. But when a local sports team wins a championship, he feels good, and planning a trip to a sun-drenched destination (on his travel agent's advice) helps him to hang in there. In any case, nothing can rouse reason from its slumber when it is time to punch in at 9 a.m. He may not be completely happy, but he will make it his business to say that he is. The third figure is the zealous mediocre person. He is truly a blight—always asking for more. This is a person who knows all the tricks; he wakes up wondering what shady ploys he can devise to win the favour of an authority whose point of view he will certainly be found to share at exactly the right moment. He also thinks about how to eliminate any competitor who might get in his way. A master of scheming, he is sustained by the art of not being deeply convinced of anything, which means he is always available to be part of any lineup dictated by circumstance. He is a mirror of his time, and the future belongs to him. Nothing will stop him—a proverb will provide him with a semblance of morality at every stage of his trajectory. His most important strength is to be completely incapable of reflexive thought. The fourth figure is the person who is mediocre in spite of herself. She does not conceal from herself, in any way, the sterile nature of what she does, or even the genuine harm her work may cause if she works in a field such as big industry, monoculture, extractivism, law, or organizational psychology. She has mouths to feed and a mortgage to pay. Doing her job under duress, yet also with shame, and well aware of the banality of evil that it represents, she also experiences, as an everyday burden, the evil of banality. At best, she will find a way to be active within a labour union or to help run a charity, until she eventually encounters in these environments the same problems as in her department. She keeps going in a state of profound uneasiness. Finally, a small number of foolhardy hotheads make up the last emblematic category: these are the people who charge forward, denouncing the workings of institutions of power, and whose only wage is the pride of not participating in them. A resistance fighter will present himself as the scourge of mediocracy until the star system one day brings him in as a member of the supporting cast, recognizing him as a candidate who might politely fill an important office: the figure of the damned.

§24

It is a passionate appeal from the heart rather than a question. "Yes, but what can *I* do about it?" It is heard, without fail, at the end of any public talk on the evils of our time. Most of the world's ecosystems are under threat, and oil companies are mafia-like "economies" more powerful than any state. Media productions are designed to manipulate us on the basis of neurological experiments. Species are disappearing. A continent of discarded plastic is forming in the Pacific, and tensions are inexorably rising in areas of geopolitical conflict throughout the world. But the question arising in response to this actually forestalls any possible answer. It goes like this:

"What can I do, Petit Chose, poor Little Nothing,* trapped in my sterile individuality, forced to eat frozen pizza in my half-basement apartment because of the high unemployment rate, rising rents, police brutality, and all the money I owe?" This is a rhetorical question, meaning: please confirm that I can't do anything about this, for I don't believe that I'm up to the act of resistance that the situation calls for. Firmly ensconced in a corner, this character pitifully asks: Where is the De Gaulle whose appeal I might answer, the Gandhi we might all follow? And indeed, at this stage of political dereliction, what can we do? "What is to be done?" is a question that once resonated as an exclamation; it was the prelude to strategic thinking about a new order. Today's individualist version, "Yes, but what can *I* do about it?" tells us that the person asking it has no hope for action: like Petit Chose, we can't do anything worthwhile. This impoverished question reveals the state to which the system has reduced us. And yet, in an underlying way, the question does raise our social and political awareness. It is the ground zero from which we can articulate our reasons to escape from ourselves, look for ways of acting on the collective structures that condition us, and understand to what extent the thing we hastily call "individual conscience" is essentially the product of a given cultural, social, and ideological context. Alphonse Daudet's

---

* *Le Petit Chose* (1868) is an autobiographical novel, variously translated as *Little Good-for-Nothing* (1878) and *Little What's-His-Name* (1898), in which French author Alphonse Daudet relates the loneliness and poverty of his difficult youth.—CB

nineteenth-century character, Petit Chose, believes himself to be utterly overwhelmed by the misfortunes of his time. He refers to himself in the third person, not out of pride, but as a way of feeling sorry for the person he claims to be: one who has no control over the woes that fatally afflict him, especially when he believes that he has found something to comfort his wounded heart. He is resigned to forgetting the gestures and initiatives that might radically change his fate. How can we explain that we are in such a static position in a world where the most terrible catastrophes have been foreseen for decades? "Poor Little Nothing, what can *I* do about it?" Stop getting indignant and move on to the next question; work relentlessly to bring about a synthesis of valid causes; organize with others beyond cliques and sectarian withdrawal; mock ideology; reduce the terms that propaganda wants to write into the core of our subjectivity to mere objects of thought; transcend hegemonic ways of organizing; see if you can establish structures that look like us. Get radical!

NOTES

INTRODUCTION

1   Robert Musil, *The Man Without Qualities*, tr. Sophie Wilkins (New York: Vintage International, 1996), 1, 57.

2   Karl Marx, *Wage Labour and Capital*, www.marxists.org.

3   Karl Marx, *A Contribution to the Critique of Political Economy*, Appendix 1.3: "The Methods of Political Economy," tr. S.W. Ryazanskaya (Moscow: Progress Publishers), www.marxists.org.

4   Translation adapted from Jean de la Bruyère, *The Characters*, 39, tr. Henri Van Laun, Project Gutenberg ebook, www.gutenberg.org.

5   Gustave Flaubert, "Préface aux *Dernières chansons* de Louis Bouilhet," http://flaubert.univ-rouen.fr (our translation).

6   Laurence J. Peter and Raymond Hull, *The Peter Principle* (Cutchogue, New York: Buccaneer Books, 1969), 45.

7   Hans Magnus Enzensberger, "In Praise of the Illiterate," tr. Martin Chalmers, in *Zig Zag: The Politics of Culture and Vice Versa* (New York: The Free Press, 1997), 281.

8   Enzensberger, "In Praise of the Illiterate," 280.

9   C.Z. Koval, M.R. Vandellen, G.M. Fitzsimons, and K.W. Ranby, "The Burden of Responsibility: Interpersonal Costs of High Self-Control," *Journal of Personality and Social Psychology* 108,5 (May 2015), 750–66.

10   Alexander Zinoviev, *The Yawning Heights*, tr. Gordon Clough (London, Sydney, and Toronto: The Bodley Head, 1979), 279.

11   Zinoviev, *Yawning Heights*, 281.

12   Edward W. Said, *Representations of the Intellectual: The 1993 Reith Lectures* (New York: Vintage Books, 1996), 73–74.

13   Said, *Representations of the Intellectual*, 74.

CHAPTER I. "KNOWLEDGE" AND EXPERTISE

1   Chris Hedges, *Empire of Illusion: The End of Literacy and the Triumph of Spectacle* (Toronto: Alfred A. Knopf Canada, 2009), 90.

2   Hedges, *Empire of Illusion*, 93–94.

3   Max Weber, "Science as Vocation," in *From Max Weber: Essays in Sociology*, ed. and tr. H.H. Gerth and C. Wright Mills (New York: Oxford University Press, 1946), 129–56.

4   Libero Zuppiroli, *La bulle universitaire: Faut-il poursuivre le rêve américain?* (Lausanne: Éditions d'En Bas, 2010) (our translation).

5   Lisa-Marie Gervais, "Malade, l'université?," *Le Devoir*, March 10, 2012 (our translation).

6   Georg Simmel, "The Concept and Tragedy of Culture," tr. Mark Ritter and David Frisby, in *Simmel on Culture: Selected Writings*, ed. David Frisby and Mike Featherstone (London, Thousand Oaks and New Delhi: SAGE Publications, 1997), 55–75.

7   Simmel, "The Concept and Tragedy of Culture," 60.

8   Simmel, "The Concept and Tragedy of Culture," 71.

9   Edelman, "Strategic Plan: Québec," May 20, 2014, www.greenpeace.org/canada, 25.

10   Greenpeace Canada, "Leaked Documents Show TransCanada Planning Dirty Tricks Campaign to Support Energy East Pipeline," Nov. 18, 2014, www.greenpeace.org/canada.

11   Éric Eugène, *Le lobbying est-il une imposture?* (Paris: Cherche-Midi, 2002) (our translation).

12   Enzensberger, "In Praise of the Illiterate," 279–80.

13   Gilles Deleuze, *Two Regimes of Madness*, ed. David Lapoujade, tr. Ames Hodges and Mike Taormina (New York: Semiotext(e), 2006), 369.

14   C. Wright Mills, *White Collar: The American Middle Classes* (New York: Oxford University Press, 1953), 151.

15   Hedges, *Empire of Illusion*, 90.

16   Kristen R. Ghodsee, "Ethnographers as Writers: A Light-Hearted Introduction to

Academese," *Savage Minds: Notes and Queries in Anthropology* (blog), https://savageminds.org, Jan. 4, 2015.

17 Steven Pinker, "Why Academics Stink at Writing," *Chronicle of Higher Education*, Sept. 26, 2014.

18 Marshall McLuhan, *The Mechanical Bride: Folklore of Industrial Man* (Berkeley: Gingko Press, 2002), 102–103.

19 McLuhan, *Mechanical Bride*, 126.

20 McLuhan, *Mechanical Bride*, 128.

21 McLuhan, *Mechanical Bride*, 128.

22 McLuhan, *Mechanical Bride*, 128.

23 McLuhan, *Mechanical Bride*, 128.

24 McLuhan, *Mechanical Bride*, 128.

25 Marie Bénilde, *On achète bien les cerveaux: La publicité et les médias* (Paris: Liber / Raison d'agir, 2008).

26 Alexandre Afonso, "How Academia Resembles a Drug Gang," LES Impact Blog, http://blogs.lse.ac.uk/impactofsocialsciences, Dec.11, 2013.

27 Marie-Ève Maillé, "Ma réaction à la table ronde sur le doctorat envoyé à l'équipe de *Médium large*," letter published on social media, May 20, 2015 (our translation).

28 Tiphaine Rivière, *Carnets de thèse* (Paris: Éditions du Seuil, 2015).

29 Afonso, "How Academia Resembles a Drug Gang."

30 Mohamed Harfi, *Les difficultés d'insertion professionnelle des docteurs*, Bureau du premier ministre de la République française, Commissariat général à la stratégie et à la prospective, Oct. 2013, www.letudiant.fr.

31 Paul Allen Anderson, "'The Game Is the Game': Tautology and Allegory in *The Wire*," *Criticism* 52,3–4 (Summer–Fall 2010).

32 Varlam Shalamov, *Ocherki prestupnogo mira* (Sketches of the Criminal World), https://shalamov.ru. This paragraph was translated from the Russian by John Woodsworth.

33 Michel Seymour, *Une idée de l'université* (Montreal: Éditions du Boréal, 2013).

34 Jean-François Cloutier, "Des placements offshore hantent l'Université de Montréal," *Journal de Montréal*, April 13, 2014 (our translation).

35 Marina Walker Guevara et al., "OffshoreLeaks: Révélations sur l'argent caché des 'princes rouges' chinois," *Le Monde*, Jan. 21, 2014.

36 Christian Rappaz, "Affaire Giroud: Les dessous d'un scandale," *L'Illustré*, March 12, 2014 (our translation).

37 Abdou Semmar, "Les affaires louches de Sonatrach aux Îles Vierges britanniques," *Algérie-Focus*, Feb. 19, 2013.

38   François Lachance, "La caisse du RRUM obtient un rendement exceptionnel," *Forum*, Nov. 9, 1998 (our translation).

39   "Le risque fiduciaire," *Zone libre*, Radio-Canada, Jan. 30, 2004.

40   Ed Pilkington, "Top US Universities Use Offshore Funds to Grow Their Huge Endowments," *Guardian*, Nov. 8, 2017; Luke Harding and Richard Adams, "Paradise Papers: Oxford and Cambridge Invested Tens of Millions Offshore," *Guardian*, Nov. 8, 2017; Robert Cribb, "U of T's Endowment, Pension Funds Have Investments in Two Offshore Tax Havens," *Toronto Star*, Nov. 8, 2017; Stephanie Saulnov, "Endowments Boom as Colleges Bury Earnings Overseas," *New York Times*, Nov. 8, 2017; Sasha Chavkin, Emilia Diaz-Struck, and Cecile S. Gallego, "More Than 100 Universities and Colleges Included in Offshore Leaks Database," International Consortium of Investigative Journalists (ICIJ), Blog, www.icij.org, Nov. 17, 2017.

41   James L. Turk, ed., *Academic Freedom in Conflict: The Struggle over Free Speech Rights in the University* (Toronto: Lorimer, 2014).

42   Catherine Martellini, "J'ai mal à mon diplôme!," *Métro* (Montreal), Aug. 10, 2014 (our translation).

43   Justin Gillis and John Schwartz, "Deeper Ties to Corporate Cash for Doubtful Climate Researcher," *New York Times*, Feb. 21, 2015.

44   Danny Hakim, "Scientists Loved and Loathed by an Agrochemical Giant," *New York Times*, Dec. 31, 2016.

45   Anahad O'Connor, "Coca-Cola Funds Scientists Who Shift Blame for Obesity Away from Bad Diets," *New York Times*, Aug. 9, 2015.

46   Duff Wilson, "Harvard Medical School in Ethics Quandary," *New York Times*, March 2, 2009.

47   Charles Ferguson, *Inside Job*, documentary, Sony Pictures Classics, 2010; John A. Byrne, "'Inside Job' Causes Changes at Columbia," Poets&Quants, https://poetsandquants.com, May 18, 2011.

48   Luc Bonneville, "Les pressions vécues et décrites par des professeurs d'une université canadienne," *Questions de communication* 26 (2014), 197–218 (our translation).

49   Bonneville, "Les pressions vécues et décrites par des professeurs d'une université canadienne."

50   Yvon Rivard, *Aimer, enseigner* (Montreal: Éditions du Boréal, 2012) (our translation).

51   Andrée Lajoie, *Vive la recherche libre!* (Montreal: Liber, 2009) (our translation).

52   Comité d'éthique du CNRS (COMETS) and Présidence du CNRS, "La politique de l'excellence en recherche," CNRS, www.cnrs.fr, May 2014 (our translation).

53   COMETS and Présidence du CNRS, "La politique de l'excellence en recherche" (our translation).

54 "Imaginaires de l'enseignement," *Contre-jour* 33 (Summer 2014). The comments quoted are from articles by Étienne Beaulieu, Jean-François Bourgeault, Thomas Mainguy, and Sylveline Bourion.

55 Anonymous, "Academia: An Abusive Partner," *Mettre la thèse entre parenthèses* (blog), http://thesenparenthese.blogspot.ca, July 4, 2014.

56 Rivard, *Aimer, enseigner,* 11 (our translation).

57 Patrice Loraux, *Le tempo de la pensée* (Paris: Éditions du Seuil, 1993).

58 Dominique Pestre, *À contre-science: Politiques et savoirs des sociétés contemporaines* (Paris: Éditions du Seuil, 2013).

59 Kate B. Carey, et al., "Incapacitated and Forcible Rape of College Women: Prevalence across the First Year," *Journal of Adolescent Health* 56,6 (June 2015).

60 Denis de Rougemont, *Journal d'un intellectuel en chômage* (Chêne-Bourg, Switzerland: La Baconnière, 2012) (our translation).

61 Bill Readings, *The University in Ruins* (Cambridge, MA, and London: Harvard University Press, 1997), 1.

62 Jacques Rancière, *The Method of Equality: Interviews with Laurent Jeanpierre and Dork Zabunyan,* tr. Julie Rose (Cambridge, UK and Malden, MA: Polity Press, 2016).

63 Rancière, *Method of Equality,* 1–2.

64 Rancière, *Method of Equality,* 4.

65 Rancière, *Method of Equality,* 49.

66 Rancière, *Method of Equality,* 115.

67 Rancière, *Method of Equality,* 115.

68 Jean-Pierre Winter, *Transmettre (ou pas)* (Paris: Albin Michel, 2012).

69 Sigmund Freud, *A General Introduction to Psychoanalysis,* tr. G. Stanley Hall (New York: Horace Liveright, 1920), 308; quoted in French in Winter, *Transmettre (ou pas),* 19–20.

70 Friedrich Nietzsche, "Nachgelassene Fragmente Dezember 1881—Januar 1882," NF-1881, 16[19], *Digital Critical Edition of the Complete Works and Letters,* ed. Paolo D'Iorio based on the critical text by G. Colli and M. Montinari (Berlin and New York: De Gruyter, 1967—), www.nietzschesource.org (our translation); quoted in French in Winter, *Transmettre (ou pas),* 15.

71 The Babylonian Talmud, Niddah 30b, http://juchre.org; quoted in French in Winter, *Transmettre (ou pas),* 27.

72 Thomas Aquinas, *Summa Theologica,* tr. Fathers of the English Dominican Province, 1947, First Part, Question 117, www.sacred-texts.com; quoted in French in Winter, *Transmettre (ou pas),* 32.

73 Winter, *Transmettre (ou pas)*, 28 (our translation).

74 Jacques Lacan, *Le Séminaire, livre XVI: D'un Autre à l'autre, 1968–1969*, http://staferla.free.fr, 99 (our translation).

75 Lacan, *Le Séminaire, livre XVI*, 99 (our translation).

76 Jacques Lacan, *The Seminar of Jacques Lacan, Book II: The Ego in Freud's Theory and in the Technique of Psychoanalysis, 1954–1955*, ed. Jacques-Alain Miller (New York: W. W. Norton, 1988), 207.

77 Winter, *Transmettre (ou pas)* (our translation), 111.

CHAPTER 2. TRADE AND FINANCE

1 Ervin Karp, *6* (Brussels: Zones sensibles, 2013) and *5* (Brussels: Zones Sensibles, 2014).

2 Frédéric Lelièvre and François Pilet, *Krach machine: Comment les traders à haute fréquence menacent de faire sauter la Bourse* (Paris: Calmann-Lévy, 2013).

3 Ivan Macaux, *Les nouveaux loups de Wall Street* (France: Chengyu Prod and Canal+, 2015).

4 "The Father of High Trading Speaks," Commodity Trade Mantra, April 9, 2014, quoted in French in Karp, *6*, 54.

5 Karp, *6*, 66–67, (our translation).

6 Karp, *6*, 68 (our translation).

7 Karp, *5* (our translation).

8 Lelièvre and Pilet, *Krach machine* (our translation).

9 Lelièvre and Pilet, *Krach machine* (our translation).

10 Franz Kafka, *The Trial*, tr. Breon Mitchell (New York: Schocken Books, 1998), 23.

11 Éric Desrosiers, "Commande record pour Bombardier," *Le Devoir*, Nov. 28, 2012 (our translation).

12 Desrosiers, "Commande record pour Bombardier"; Bombardier, "VistaJet Thinks Global with $7.8 Billion Bombardier Business Aircraft Order," press release, http://ir.bombardier.com, Nov. 27, 2012.

13 Niall McCarthy, "The Countries Where Private Jet Ownership Is Soaring," *Forbes*, www.forbes.com, March 2, 2017.

14 Desrosiers, "Commande record pour Bombardier" (our translation).

15 Capgemini and Merrill Lynch, *World Wealth Report 2007*, www.capgemini.com.

16 Desrosiers, "Commande record pour Bombardier" (our translation).

17 David Rothkopf, *Superclass: The Global Power Elite and the World They Are Making* (Toronto: Viking Canada, 2008).

18 Rothkopf, *Superclass*, 24.

19 Rothkopf, *Superclass*, 25.

20 Thomas Gerbet, "De mystérieux hommes d'affaires chinois veulent s'établir au Québec et changer les règles," Radio-Canada, April 28, 2015; Radio-Canada, "Un millier de gens d'affaires chinois à Varennes?," Aug. 13, 2015.

21 Claude-André Mayrand, "Laval intéresse les Chinois: Un centre de commerce mondial et un 'Chinatown' de luxe dans l'ancien ciné-parc," *Journal de Montréal,* Nov. 27, 2013 (our translation).

22 Alain Deneault, *Canada: A New Tax Haven*, tr. Catherine Browne (Vancouver: Talonbooks, 2015).

23 Radio-Canada, "Corruption à grande echelle," http://ici.radio-canada.ca, March 4, 2013.

24 Radio-Canada, "L'éthique peut triompher sans que PKP vende ses actions, estime Michel Nadeau," Oct. 8, 2014 (our translation).

25 Baltasar Gracián, *El Criticón*, Instituto Nacional de Tecnologías Educativas y de Formación del Profesorado, http://educalab.es/intef, 122 (our translation).

26 Andrea Dworkin, *Right-Wing Women* (New York: G.P. Putnam's Sons, Perigee Books, 1983), 13.

27 Georg Simmel, "The Crisis of Culture," tr. D.E. Jenkinson, in *Simmel on Culture: Selected Writings*, ed. David Frisby and Mike Featherstone (London, Thousand Oaks and New Delhi: Sage Publications, 1997), 97.

28 Georg Simmel, *The Philosophy of Money*, ed. David Frisby, tr. Tom Bottomore and David Frisby (London and New York: Routledge, 2004), 232.

29 Simmel, *Philosophy of Money*, 242.

30 Simmel, *Philosophy of Money*, 244.

31 Simmel, *Philosophy of Money*, 246.

32 Simmel, *Philosophy of Money*, 256.

33 Simmel, *Philosophy of Money*, 66.

34 Simmel, *Philosophy of Money*, 257.

35 Simmel, *Philosophy of Money*, 255.

36 Sanou Mbaye, *L'Afrique au secours de l'Afrique* (Ivry-sur-Seine: Éditions de l'Atelier, 2009).

37 Johanna Siméant, *Contester au Mali: Formes de la mobilisation et de la critique à Bamako* (Paris: Karthala, 2014).

38 *The Wanted 18*, dir. Paul Cowan and Amer Shomali (National Film Board of Canada, 2014).

39 Dev Kar and Sarah Freitas, *Illicit Financial Flows from Developing Countries, 2001–2010*, Global Financial Integrity, Washington, DC, Dec. 2012.

40 Fritz Deshommes, "Haïti: Quelle refondation?," in *Refonder Haïti?*, ed. Pierre Buteau, Rodney Saint-Éloi, and Lyonel Trouillot (Montreal: Mémoire d'encrier, 2011) (our translation).

41 Justin Podur, *Haiti's New Dictatorship: The Coup, the Earthquake and the UN Occupation* (Toronto: Between the Lines, 2012).

42 Nikolas Barry-Shaw and Dru Oja Jay, *Paved with Good Intentions: Canada's Development NGOs from Idealism to Imperialism* (Halifax and Winnipeg: Fernwood Publishing, 2012).

43 Raoul Peck, *Fatal Assistance*, Velvet Film, 2013.

44 Jacques Roumain, *Masters of the Dew*, tr. Langston Hughes and Mercer Cook (London: Heinemann Educational Books, 1986).

45 "Majescor to Acquire Interest in a Strategic Gold-Copper Property in Haiti," press release, www.marketwired.com, April 23, 2009.

46 Hugo Fontaine, "Haïti: Un trésor sous les ruines?," *La Presse*, Montreal, Oct. 21, 2012 (our translation).

47 Fontaine, "Haïti: Un trésor sous les ruines?" (our translation).

48 Ayiti Kale Je, "Le parc industriel de Caracol: À qui profitera le pari?," Plateforme Haïtienne de Plaidoyer pour un Développement Alternatif, http://papda.org, March 9, 2013.

49 "Le Sénat vote la suspension des permis miniers en Haïti," *Haïti Libre*, www.haitilibre.com, Feb. 21, 2013 (our translation).

50 Erwin Wagenhofer, *Let's Make Money* (Austria, 2009).

51 Ghislaine Raymond, *Le partenariat social: Sommet socio-économique de 1996, syndicats et groupes populaires* (Montreal: M Éditeur, 2013).

52 Jean-Marie Pernot, *Syndicats: Lendemains de crise?* (Paris: Gallimard, 2010).

53 Raymond, *Le partenariat social* (our translation).

54 Rachida El Azzouzi, "Jean-Marie Pernot: 'La démocratie sociale à la française est un échec'," *Médiapart*, www.snuaquitaine.fr, May 26, 2015.

55 Mills, *White Collar*, xii.

56 Mills, *White Collar*, xvi.

57 "McDonald's: Appel à la 'mobilisation mondiale' de syndicats français et américains," *Le Devoir*, Jan. 15, 2016; NUPGE, "About the All Together Now! Campaign,"

https://alltogethernow.nupge.ca; AFL-CIO, "100 Organizations Urge Congress to Reject Giant Tax Loophole for Offshoring and Tax Avoidance," press release, Oct. 2, 2017.

58 Gabriel Tarde, *Psychologie économique*, Vol. 1 (Paris: Félix Alcan, 1902) (our translation).

59 Walter Benjamin, "Critique of Violence," in *Reflections: Essays, Aphorisms, Autobiographical Writings*, ed. Peter Demetz, tr. Edmund Jephcott (New York: Schocken Books, 1986), 282.

CHAPTER 3. CULTURE AND CIVILIZATION

1 Sigmund Freud, *Jokes and Their Relation to the Unconscious*, tr. James Strachey (New York: W.W. Norton & Co., 1963), 16.

2 Freud, *Jokes and Their Relation to the Unconscious*, 17.

3 Pierre Falardeau, *Le temps des bouffons*, 1985 (our translation).

4 Andreas Pichler, *The Venice Syndrome*, National Film Board of Canada, 2012.

5 Freud, *Jokes and Their Relation to the Unconscious*, 20.

6 Hans Magnus Enzensberger, "Der Triumph der Bild-Zeitung oder die Katastrophe der Pressefreiheit," *Merkur* 37,420 (June 1983), 656 (our translation).

7 The combined value of assets held by a Desmarais family trust and the two Desmarais brothers, André and Paul Jr., was estimated to be $4.1 billion in 2017. See Jean-François Cloutier, "Comment les Desmarais ont évité le classement Forbes," *Journal de Montréal*, March 25, 2017.

8 Peter Charles Newman, "Epitaph for the Two-Party State," *Maclean's*, Nov. 1, 1993, 14.

9 Matt Lundy, "The Life of Paul Desmarais: From Bus Operator to Connected Billionaire," *Globe and Mail*, Oct. 9, 2013.

10 Anonymous Québec, "The Making Of." This untitled and undated video, shot in 2008 (line producer: Oxygène, creative team: Paul Desmarais, Studio JP Molyneux and Les Ensembliers), was released by the Anonymous movement in 2012 (https://youtu.be/M7OlFp_9U_E.)

11 Theodor Adorno and Max Horkheimer, "The Culture Industry: Enlightenment as Mass Deception," in *Dialectic of Enlightenment*, tr. John Cumming (New York: Continuum, 1989), 121.

12 Adorno and Horkheimer, "The Culture Industry," 129.

13   Herbert Marcuse, *One-Dimensional Man: Studies in the Ideology of Advanced Industrial Society*, 2nd ed. (London and New York: Routledge, 2002), 10.

14   Quoted in "Extrait de la politique culturelle de Liza Frulla," *Liberté* 303 (Spring 2014), 31 (our translation).

15   This is our translation of an expression used by the Board of Trade in French: "créateurs d'affaires." In English, the Board of Trade uses the expression "the art of business."

16   Board of Trade of Metropolitan Montreal, "The Art of Investing in Culture. A Guide for Businesspeople," www.artsmontreal.org, 2011; "Leave a Legacy", n.d., www.montrealartsaffaires.org.

17   Stéphane Mallarmé, "Gold," in *Divagations*, tr. Barbara Johnson (Cambridge, MA: Harvard University Press, 2007), 255.

18   Gertrude Stein, "Money," in *On the Third Hand: Humor in the Dismal Science*, ed. Caroline Postelle Clotfelter (Ann Arbor: University of Michigan Press, 1996), 236.

19   Joseph Beuys, *What Is Money?*, tr. Isabelle Boccon-Gibod (Forest Row: Clairview Books, 2010).

20   Antonin Artaud, "La faim n'attend pas . . ." (1931–1932), *Œuvres complètes*, 8 (Paris: Gallimard, 1971), our translation.

21   André Gide, *The Counterfeiters*, tr. Dorothy Bussy (New York: Vintage Books, 1973), 149.

22   Gide, *The Counterfeiters*, 149. We have changed the English translation somewhat in order to follow the original more closely.

23   Gilbert White, *The Natural History and Antiquities of Selborne*, Letter VIII (London: John Van Voorst, 1877), 23.

24   René Char, "Man Flees Suffocation," tr. Mary Ann Caws, in *Selected Poems*, ed. Mary Ann Caws and Tina Jolas (New York: New Directions, 1992), 17.

25   Marie-Josée Mondzain, *Image, Icon, Economy: The Byzantine Origins of the Contemporary Imaginary*, tr. Rico Franses (Stanford, CA: Stanford University Press, 2004).

26   Richard Avenarius, *Philosophie als Denken der Welt gemäß dem Prinzip des kleinsten Kraftmaßes: Prolegomena zu einer Kritik der reinen Erfahrung* (Leipzig: Fues's Verlag [R. Reisland]), 1876.

27   Transportation Safety Board of Canada, *Lac-Mégantic Runaway Train and Derailment Investigation Summary* (Ottawa: Public Works and Government Services Canada, 2014), 7.

28   Anne-Marie Saint-Cerny, "Les tragédies sans fin de Lac-Mégantic," *À babord* 68 (Feb.–March 2017).

29   Jacques McNish, Grant Robertson, and Kim Mackrael, "Crude That Exploded in

Lac-Mégantic Was Mislabelled: Officials," *Globe and Mail*, Sept. 11, 2013.

30 Transportation Safety Board of Canada, *Statistical Summary—Railway Occurrences 2016*, www.bst-tsb.gc.ca, Dec. 7, 2017; Statistics Portal, "Number of Rail Accidents and Incidents in the United States from 2013 to 2016," www.statista.com.

31 Transportation Safety Board of Canada, *Lac-Mégantic Runaway Train and Derailment Investigation Summary*, 3.

32 Les Whittington et al., "Lac Megantic Explosion: Ottawa Approved Having Only One Engineer on Ill-Fated Train," *Toronto Star*, July 9, 2013.

33 Melanie Marquis, "Study Shows High Pollution at Lac-Mégantic: One Carcinogen 394,444 Times above Limit," *Globe and Mail*, Aug. 13, 2013.

34 Gilles Lipovetsky and Jean Serroy, *L'esthétisation du monde: Vivre à l'âge du capitalisme artiste* (Paris: Gallimard, 2013), 34 (our translation).

35 Radio-Canada, "Reconstruction de Lac-Mégantic: Des travailleurs critiquent la gestion des travaux," Oct. 23, 2013.

36 Günther Anders, *Die Antiquiertheit des Menschen: Über die Seeleim Zeitalter der zweiten industriellen Revolution* (Munich: Verlag C. H. Beck, 1956), 102. All quotes from Anders have been translated from the German by Diana Halfpenny.

37 Anders, 118.

38 Anders, 161.

39 Mikel Dufrenne, *Subversion perversion* (Paris: Presses universitaires de France, 1977).

40 See, for example, "The Container Post," Architechnophilia (blog), http://architechnophilia.blogspot.ca, March 10, 2009, "Containers 2.0," March 31, 2009.

CHAPTER 4. REVOLUTION

1 Albert Camus, *Resistance, Rebellion and Death: Essays*, tr. Justin O'Brien (New York: Vintage International, 1988), 249.

2 Rosa Luxemburg, *The Essential Rosa Luxemburg: Reform or Revolution and The Mass Strike*, tr. Integer and Patrick Lavin (Chicago: Haymarket Books, 2008).

3 Patrice Loraux, *Le tempo de la pensée* (Paris: Seuil, 1993) (our translation).

4 Aristotle, *De generatione et corruptione*, 317a20, tr. C.J.F. Williams (Oxford: Clarendon Press, 1982), 8.

5 Aristotle, *De generatione et corruptione*, 319a20, 13.

6 Aristotle, *De generatione et corruptione*, 319a15, 13.

EPILOGUE

"The Politics of the Extreme Centre" is partly based on reworkings of excerpts from the following publications: "Le spectre politique," *L'Inconvénient* 65 (Summer 2016); "Le prolétariat en négatif," in *Médias et minorités*, a collection edited in fall 2016 by the online publication *L'esprit libre;* three columns published in *Liberté*: "Qu'est-ce que je peux faire?" 311 (Spring 2016), "Autour de Dieu," 312 (Summer 2016), "Le 11 novembre 2015," 313 (Fall 2016).

1 Saskia Sassen, *Territory, Authority, Rights: From Medieval to Global Assemblages* (Princeton, NJ: Princeton University Press, 2007).

2 Hans Magnus Enzensberger's novel *Der kurze Sommer der Anarchie* (Frankfurt: Suhrkampf Verlag, 1972) is available online in English at https://libcom.org.

3 Pierre Serna, *La République des girouettes: 1789–1815 et au-delà* (Paris: Champ Vallon, 2005) (our translation).

4 David Revault d'Allonnes, "François Hollande lance l'opération réhabilitation," *Le Monde*, May 3, 2016.

5 Éric Bédard, "Être conservateur aujourd'hui," *L'Inconvénient* (Summer 2016) (our translation).

6 Dealbook, "Blankfein Says He's Just Doing 'God's Work,'" *New York Times*, https://dealbook.nytimes.com, Nov. 9, 2009.

7 Jesper Kunde, *Corporate Religion* (London: Financial Times and Prentice Hall, 2002). The quote appears in most online descriptions of the book.

8 Marie-Claude Élie-Morin, *La dictature du bonheur* (Montréal: VLB Éditeur, 2015).

9 Chavie Lieber, "The Self-Help Movement Behind Lululemon's Eerie Dogma," *Racked*, www.racked.com, Jan. 9, 2014.

10 Friedrich Nietzsche, *Thus Spoke Zarathustra*, part 3, tr. Graham Parkes (Oxford: Oxford University Press, 2005), 147.

11 Luc Boltanski, *Mysteries and Conspiracies: Detective Stories, Spy Novels and the Making of Modern Societies*, tr. Catherine Porter (Cambridge, UK: Polity Press, 2014), chapter 5.

12 Michel Foucault, *Discipline and Punish*, tr. Alan Sheridan (New York: Vintage Books, 1995), 135.

13 Mats Alvesson and André Spicer, "A Stupidity-Based Theory of Organizations," *Journal of Management Studies* 49, 7 (Nov. 2012), 1194.

14 Alvesson and Spicer, "A Stupidity-Based Theory of Organizations," 1197, citing James G. March, "Learning to Be Risk Averse," *Psychological Review* 103 (1996),

308–319, and "Rationality, Foolishness, and Adaptive Intelligence," *Strategic Management Journal* 27 (2006), 201–21.

15 Pierre Lefebvre, *Confessions d'un cassé* (Montréal: Éditions du Boréal, 2015).

16 Georges Perec, *A Man Asleep*, tr. Andrew Leak (Boston: David R. Godine, 1990).

17 Lefebvre, *Confessions d'un cassé*, 62 (our translation).